Endor

A superb and deeply insightful book. What Deborah and Barak in the Bible accomplished for their nation through military means, we as God's people can now accomplish through prayerful action as we find His strategy for our nation. Through biblical examples and personal testimony, Brenda VanWinkle masterfully takes the reader on a journey to find hope through our Heavenly Father.

Darryl K. Ahner
PhD, LTC, U.S. Army retired

In *An Unclouded Sun*, my beloved friend, Brenda VanWinkle, has struck a cord releasing harmonic resonance within one's soul. How desperately every follower of Jesus Christ, needs hope to rise up within them to drive out the despair that continually assaults our minds and hearts today.

Brenda's grasp of the scriptures and anointed teaching gift coupled with her ability to put you "into the story" ignites hope for today and a sense of purpose for tomorrow.

Richard (Dick) Dungan
Rejoice Ministries International, Norfolk, NB

I love to read books by people I personally know because even with allegories or fiction you still see the true heart of the author. Brenda has a heart to impart hope to the body of Christ. She does that very effectively in her new book *An Unclouded Sun*. It was easy to relate to this book. Living with an adventurous person for most of my life caused my own personal desires to be squelched for years while longing for more. Brenda takes us through an amazing journey of finding hope to live your dreams and discover your life's song. As a person who has had to redefine her life's song and discover her personal journey of hope Brenda's book encouraged me to go even further. This book is an enjoyable read that imparts hope to do the impossible. Thanks Brenda. You are a real gift to the body.

Trisha Frost
Co-Founder Shiloh Place Ministries, Conway, SC

An Unclouded Sun brings hope to the generations. Brenda Van Winkle shares her testimony of hope from her life and how our lives parallel Deborah from Judges 4. Deborah restored hope when the streets were not safe to dwell in. Brenda gives us hope that we can we can do the same. Her book will awaken you and give you courage to hope again. It will encourage you to look more closely at Gods hand in all of creation. I can see more clearly since reading *An Unclouded Sun*. Thank you Brenda for awakening us!

Lucy Riethmiller
President, Deborah Company Midwest Region, Buffalo, MN

Brenda Van Winkle ably retells Deborah's story and shares insights, which reveal her understanding of the Scriptures and truths beyond the obvious.

In this book we are offered an understanding of the hope that is ours because of the Father's love for us; Hope for this generation, hope for today and tomorrow.

It is more than just a good read, it is a *must* read.

Iverna Tompkins

an unclouded Sun

BRENDA D. VANWINKLE

© copyright 2012 Brenda VanWinkle
P.O. Box 494624
Redding, California 96049

Cover Graphics, Interior Design and Formatting
by Lorraine Box PropheticArt@sbcglobal.net

Edited by Jo Robbins, AfterWords brownrobbins@att.net

© copyright 2012 All rights reserved. This book is protected by the copyright laws of the United States of America. This book may not be copied or reprinted for commercial gain or profit. The use of short quotations or occasional page copying for personal or group study is permitted. Permission will be granted upon request.

Scripture taken from the New American Standard Bible®, Copyright © 1960, 1962, 1963, 1968, 1971, 1972, 1973, 1975, 1977, 1995 by The Lockman Foundation. Used by permission.

Scripture taken from the New King James Version. Copyright © 1982 by Thomas Nelson, Inc. Used by permission. All rights reserved.

The Holy Bible, New International Version® NIV® Copyright © 1973, 1978, 1984, 2010 by Biblica, Inc™ Used by permission. All rights reserved worldwide.

Scripture taken from The Message. Copyright © 1993 ,1994, 1995, 1996, 2000, 2001, 2002. Used by permission of NavPress Publishing Group.

The Holy Bible, English Standard Version (ESV) is adapted from the Revised Standard Version of the Bible, Copyright Division of Christian Education of the National Council of the Churches of Christ in the U.S.A. All rights reserved.

Dedication

For my husband, Jim.
For my children and grandchildren.
My heart is yours.
Live bravely. Love fully.
Live free.

Dedicated to my sister,
the most amazing Deborah I know.

In honor and loving memory of my Mom,
Jane Elizabeth Williams Dixon.
Even now, you are my inspiration.

Contents

Forward	xi	Paul Manwaring
Poem	xiii	
Introduction	xv	
Honey On My Lips	1	chapter one
Those Who Have Songs To Sing	13	chapter two
Pursuing Destiny	27	chapter three
Named With Purpose And Hope	39	chapter four
Against All Odds	51	chapter five
Securing Our Position	63	chapter six
Tuning In To God's Voice	75	chapter seven
We Need A Bigger Tent	89	chapter eight
Walking In Hope	101	chapter nine
The Community We Live In	113	chapter ten
An Unclouded Sun	127	chapter eleven
The Unstoppable Song Of Hope	139	chapter twelve
Epilogue	147	
Resources	151	
Other Titles by Brenda	153	

Forward

As soon as I began to read this book, I experienced memories and thoughts being stirred up within me. I love books that do this. This is a book that will both encourage you with what is written, but will also remind you of your own memories, stories, and testimonies through which you can also find encouragement!

This book could easily be titled Finding Your Song. What songs do best is what the early pages of this book did for me: evoked a memory and began to sing an encouraging melody to me.

The first memory this book brought to mind was of a lady I met whose niece had just been told her unborn baby was hydrocephalic (water on the brain). I prayed with her and gave her a word from God that the family should name the baby. Little did I know that the lady's brother, the grandfather-to-be, composed songs over each of his grand-children. The song that would be composed for this unborn baby was to be a supernatural song of hope. I learned later that the baby was named Judah, and he was born completely healthy!

Much like that song sung over an unborn baby, I believe that this book will sing over you and bring you identity, hope, and purpose. The things yet to be born will come to life within you and bring forth life and health.

The chapter titled "Unstoppable Song of Hope" is the song everyone needs to hear—the song that so many are desperately searching for in our world today. Hope, when found, is unstoppable. Paul says in Romans 5, "Hope does not disappoint." This book is a call to not just—in the words of the author—have a message, but live a message. A lived out message has the power to transform the world around you.

The other reminder I received while reading this book was a phrase I wrote some years ago: "Hope is the sketch on the canvas which invites the master painter to complete the painting." This book will cause you to get your pencils and paper out and start sketching.

So many of my favorite bible characters are unveiled in this book in such a way that makes hope tangible for everyone, and not simply the vantage point of the unreachable "great" saints. Hope is for all of us who are indeed the saints that all of scripture writes about.

Throughout the reading of this book, hope's diluted meaning—of being about chance—will be erased, and replaced with real meaning. Diluted hope has made it essential that true hope be rediscovered. My favorite verse in the book of Job is 5:16, "When the helpless find hope, unrighteousness must shut its mouth." What power hope has! What power this book has! When unrighteousness is silenced, there is only one voice: the voice of righteousness.

This book, this song of hope, will silence the lyrics of hopelessness and replace them with hope: hope in who you are and what you are alive for. It will release the song of righteousness in your life, family, and sphere of influence

Paul Manwaring

Author of *What On Earth Is Glory*
and *Kisses From A Good God* (to be released October 1, 2012)

*Hope. Hope. Hope. Hope.
Hope is your lifeline.
Hope is the abiding pressure of Presence
that will keep you heading toward your goal.*

*Your dream is not too big. Hope.
The longing is able to be fulfilled. Hope.
What you now consider a huge, out-there goal
will one day be a historical fact and a Kingdom reality.
Keep hoping.*

*It's time. It's time to believe bigger than ever before,
to rejoice higher and deeper
than you've ever known joy before,
to pull on your courage and go for the gold.*

*Don't stop hoping.
Hope remains. Hope does not disappoint.*

Introduction

Few things captivate the imagination like a full moon. Legends are written and songs sung about them, and in all the eons gone by, humankind has looked to the night sky, in awe of the splendor of lights displayed there. I am with abundant company when I am amazed at how a full moon lights up an otherwise black night.

Yet as glorious as it is, the fullest of moons cannot begin to compare to a sunrise. Whether we remain awake throughout a sleepless night or a night of celebration, the glimmer of hope that sunrise brings with the breaking of dawn lets us know: today is a new start. Hope is rising like the dawn, and God's brand new mercy will light my path this day.

The miracle of sunrise is hope. The promise of the Lord is that, day after day, as long as life on earth continues, the sun will rise in the morning. (Genesis 8:22)

My purpose in writing this book is to express what I've learned about hope — hope as dependable as the sunrise and as sure as the dawn. I have read thousands of books in my lifetime (at least it seems) and heard as many sermons. Many of them have taught me about the Christian faith and God's love. Very few have given me insight or understanding of hope. I have attempted to bring that understanding in these pages. I have demonstrated, using Biblical texts and personal stories, that hope is both present and attainable, no matter how difficult or trying one's circumstance.

"We live in a day of great anxiety and terror." That statement or one with the same meaning is spoken or implied often these days. Yet looking back through the history of our human existence, has there ever been a time when this has not been true? I propose not. In whatever time God ordains a person to live, that person must face fear and hopelessness in one way or another. (Acts 17:26)

Perhaps that is one of the reasons Holy Spirit inspired Paul to state clearly in 1Corinthians 13:13 that faith, hope, and love will all remain. Remain forever. For always. Throughout the joys and trials of each generation. Many of us have been taught and believe that Love will remain, for God is love. The 1990's brought a heavy emphasis on faith teaching. Faith will always be, as Jesus is our faith. He is the author and finisher of it (Hebrews 12:2), and He is the substance of what we hoped for.

Where does that leave hope itself?

While I have lived my life with great anticipation of good, my understanding of hope — the nature and substance of it — was reduced to a pie-in-the-sky wish, a dream of something I couldn't quite lay hold of but longed to experience. Hope felt more like a birthday wish kept secret when I blew out the candles on my cake: after all, if I made my hope known, it wouldn't come true.

The Word of God tells us that the Holy Spirit enables us to have enough hope that it overflows. Romans 15:13 reads:

> "May the God of hope fill you with all joy and peace in believing, so that by the power of the Holy Spirit you may abound in hope."

Through these scriptures we see the Trinity working in divine tandem to keep faith, hope and love available to us always.

Let's face it: we live in a day of great anxiety and terror. I welcome you into this journey of exploring hope, finding hope, maintaining hope. In these pages we'll discover together that the Bible describes Jesus in terms of the rising sun, accessible and without clouds to dim the warmth of His presence. I long to know Him in this way. After all, better than a wish tossed up to the man in the moon is a relationship with One Whose lovers are like an unclouded sun.

ONE

Honey On My Lips

The bee is more honored than other animals, not because she labors, but because she labors for others.

Saint John Chrysostom

Bees deserve whatever reputation they've been given, if you ask me.

In nearly all regards, bees are honorable little creatures. Bees are beautiful, a naturally occurring engineering marvel. They are necessary: just by doing what comes naturally, they pollinate flowers, thereby providing fruits and vegetables for us. Bees are persistent. Ever try to chase one away that is fascinated by your cologne? We make movies about their lives, and the honey that they produce is one of the purest foods on the planet. To those who have worked long and hard to accomplish a goal, we offer the compliment, "You've been busy as a bee!" Most anyone who knows anything about them considers the bee a great asset to our world. Yes, bees have a wonderful reputation except for one little thing: make a bee angry and it will sting.

The Bee

Deborah was the name she'd been given. This name, which means "bee," seems to fit what we read of her. One who is busy all the time. One who gathers a little from here and a little from there to create sweetness for others to enjoy. One who, when challenged, can sting.

It seemed she had inherited from her parents the ability to look at a matter and see beyond her natural vision into another, deeper level of reality. Seeing other women her age content to raise children and take care of the home front, Deborah was confronted daily with her own dissatisfaction. While happy for their contentment, her own seemed out of reach. Life was good, and everything in her society told her she should be satisfied, but something was stirring inside of her, longing to be released. Always busy doing one project after another, Deborah soon gained a reputation as a woman to be counted on in time of need or distress. Not only did she listen to others and care for them, but she seemed to have wisdom far beyond her years and training. Deborah could see things that no one else could see, and when confronted with a problem, she had the ability to listen beyond spoken words and recognize the pain and confusion behind them. Deborah could get to the heart of the issue because Deborah knew the heart of God.

Sometimes, like a bee, her words stung as they penetrated the surface lie and exposed the motive or shame that lay covered and hidden. A happy person by nature, her quick wit was her trademark. Anyone in the vicinity of her home could hear her happily humming a tune as she kept busy, her boundless energy flowing from her lips as she sang and her hands as she served.

Yet, no matter how much she gave herself to serving others — preparing meals for the ill and elderly or lending an ear to her neighbor's woes, Deborah sensed that there was more: more for her to do, more of an impact her life was meant to make, more of her God to experience.

Deborah knew that there had to be *more*.

A Story for Today

The above description is not biblically accurate, but rather one of the scenarios I have imagined about Deborah's life, from the story of Deborah in the Bible book of Judges. I have looked for stories about Deborah in multiple bookstores, and I can tell you: she's hard to find. Looking through books specifically dedicated to telling stories of women of the Bible, I've been shocked that many of them don't mention Deborah at all, and if they do, their take on her life is weak at best. A few books specifically recount Deborah's important role as a general in the Biblical book of Judges. Many of them offer great insights about how we, too, can live in boldness and confidence, but I've never found a book specifically written to express how Deborah's life and story apply to us today in a post 9-11 world. Even though detailed information about Deborah is limited, I know this: she lived in a day when terror gripped the land. In fact, the book of Judges, Chapter 5, tells us that the people were so afraid that they traveled back roads rather than the highways, and that village life had ceased. Despite widespread fear and terrorism, Deborah was able to hear the heart of God and to understand what it would take to defeat terrorism and turn her nation back to God. Together with the leader of the armed forces and a humble ironworker's wife, Deborah defeated the Osama bin Laden of her day, and even better, played a key role in bringing revival and rest to her land. This sounds like a woman who knew something valuable that could help us here and now.

The characters in Deborah's story are worth closer examination. We can be inspired by Deborah's bravery in the face of terrorism. Barak, the general with whom she planned the enemy's defeat, is usually made out to be the wimp of the story, but we'll look at another possibility in a later chapter. And we mustn't dismiss Jael, the nomad. To describe her as "just a woman" doesn't cut it. She was, in fact, like most of us, minding her own business and living her day-to-day life when terror arrived at her door. Nothing in the story gives any indication that she was looking for a way to make a name for herself, nor does it appear that she was looking to be a heroine. Yet, in the normal course of her life, terror literally came to her house, and she had the courage and wisdom to know what to do. Today, when terror arrives — whether in the form of divorce, untimely death, sickness, runaway children, or any other — I want to learn from these three characters how to deal with it and find hope once again.

The Name Game

To say that William Shakespeare had a way with words is a bit like saying that Mt. Everest is a tall mountain – a vast understatement at best. Imagine that, like Shakespeare, the words you write would be memorized and recognized centuries later! Many years have passed since I was required to memorize passages from Shakespeare's work in high school, yet to this day I can quote passages that were profound enough to have stayed with me all these years. One such passage is from *Romeo and Juliet*. The lovers are discussing the fact that even though their families are long-time rivals, their family names should not stand in the way of their love for one another. There in this discourse is the famous line, "What's in a name? That which we call a rose by any other name would smell as sweet" (*Romeo and Juliet*, II, ii, 1-2).

I know that Shakespeare was technically right, but the fact is that roses are now associated with particular characteristics. When people hear the word "rose," they think of love and romance and a fragrance that transports them to memories associated with the pleasure of being loved. A dozen long-stemmed roses are costly, and when we think of buying or receiving a dozen long-stemmed roses, we know that a sacrifice has been made to express friendship or love. I'm sure that if I chose to call the roses planted around my house "skunk weed" or "trash essence," their perfume would not change and they would smell as sweet as they do now, but the mere mention of the name "rose" carries a world of emotion and memory and hope. I'd venture to say that if you told a friend or loved one that you were sending a gift of trash weed, the response would be quite different from the one you'd receive by announcing a gift of roses.

Names do matter.

There's Something About That Name

In the west, we don't choose our own names; They are chosen for us by our parents. It's not easy to legally change our names, either. What if you are given a name that doesn't fit you or that you don't like? What is a "good name?"

I remember being given a "new name" by my dear mentor, Pat Bailey. I met Pat when my husband Jim and I moved to Missouri to attend Bible School in the early 1980's. Much of the baggage I took with me was not in boxes or suitcases; rather, it was the junk in my emotions and soul that had been gathering over the course of my lifetime. Oh, I loved Jesus as much as I could, and I longed to be like Him. Shall we just suffice it to say that we're all on a journey toward being like Him but haven't yet arrived?

At that time, I'd always been a person who saw the world in black or white; no gray allowed. I had a strong sense of justice and clearly marked divisions between right and wrong. (Anyone with a prophetic gift knows what I'm talking about!) I knew I was too hard on myself and others but hadn't yet grown or matured enough in my own identity to deal well with these "righteous" emotions. Pat loved me as I was, and amazingly, as she began speaking life and hope to me, I began to change and heal.

One night she called me on the phone, and when I picked up she said, "Well, hello, Grace and Mercy!" I was furious! I was sure she was making fun of me (since grace and mercy were what I married in Jim, not what I'd yet become), and I hung up the phone. It wasn't long until I had Momma Pat on my doorstep. The first thing she said was never to hang up the phone on her. The second was like warm, healing honey being poured on the raw edges of my ragged identity: "I didn't call you that to mock you. I called you Grace and Mercy because God told me that's what He is forming in you." I repented, Pat forgave me, and from that day on I never forgot that God had named me something I never would have named myself.

I had new hope — hope to become someone better, something more.

My Name Means "Forgive"

Over the course of the years we have worked in Asia, Jim and I have gathered to us many whom we consider our spiritual sons and daughters, and also many who look to us as spiritual parents. Fred is one of those.

A gentle, unimposing young man, Fred behaved as though his life had been rather happy and easy. One day, as he and I were visiting at a picnic table while waiting for Jim to join us, I asked him about his name. He explained what it meant and then told me that he changed his name from the one his parents gave him at birth. Surprised by this, I asked him why.

In his own humble, honoring way, he told me bits and pieces of a childhood filled with physical beatings and verbal abuse, all at the hand and voice of his dad. Peaceful, gentle Fred was a disappointment to his dad, and often heard about it. Then one day, long before meeting Jesus, Fred heard about the concept of forgiveness and decided that it was what he must do if he were to have any peace in his mind and soul. He changed his name, he told me, so that each time he wrote it or heard it called out he would be reminded of the choice he had made. His new name defined his hope for a new beginning. The name he chose for himself: One Who Forgives Often.

Each of us was given a name by our parents, the legal name by which we are known. Yet each of us has also been called numerous other names throughout our life journey — some of them helpful and encouraging, others not so much. Our names matter. Not only do they help identify us in the minds and conversations of others, but the name we give ourselves – the way we see our own identity and name ourselves – carries a weight that either lifts or burdens our souls.

Our name, identity and purpose all come from our connection with the Father. Let your name be one that, when people hear it, brings thoughts of forgiveness and joy and hope; in essence, let your name reflect the One Whose name you carry.

The Name Above All

The Bible is filled with names for Father God and Jesus, as well as Holy Spirit. In fact, books have been written about what the various names mean in Hebrew, Greek and Aramaic. My research has revealed approximately 366 names for God. They all refer to the same God –the same Lord, the same Savior – but we've been given this many names to address, call or describe Him. Even with all the names He's been given, He cannot be fully described. He is so vast, His expressions so extravagant and His Presence so complete, that He simply can't be confined to definition.

Proverbs 18:10 talks about the Name of the Lord. It reads: "The name of the Lord is a strong tower: the righteous run to it and are safe." Imagine: a name that is a tower!

While visiting Northern Ireland a few years back, my husband and I happened upon a small stone church while driving along the winding country roads. Named Saul Church, it is believed to have been built in the location of a barn where St. Patrick once held services. Alongside the church building stands a stone tower. Not very large by modern standards, it was nonetheless a place of refuge in days gone by. When attacked by enemies, the parishioners knew what to do – run into the tower! A stone tower couldn't be burnt, and it was built substantially enough that it could not easily be knocked down. Lookouts climbed to the top of the tower to scout out the enemy's position and strength, and while the men fought the enemy and the lookouts called out strategy, the women and children stayed huddled within the safety of the tower.

I can picture being in a tower; it's not hard to imagine. As children we hear stories about Rapunzel, Beauty and numerous other heroines in their towers, but to grasp the concept of a *name* being a strong tower takes some imagination – at least until we realize that the Word isn't talking about using Jesus' name to hide from physical bullets and arrows, but rather about hiding from the schemes and deceptions of the enemy of our souls.

The knowledge that our God is vast and good gives us great hope. No matter how overwhelming our circumstance, how stunning our present difficulty or how deep our pain, we have hope personified within the greatness of His name.

As Nahum 1:7 tells us: "The Lord is good, A stronghold in the day of trouble. And He knows those who trust in Him."

Sweeter than Honey

I love Psalm 119:103: "How sweet are Your words to my taste, sweeter than honey to my mouth!" When on our lips in worship and gratitude, His very name gives our words a sweetness that makes us sound like Him. When we lick our lips, sweetened with the honey of His name, we remember to speak carefully, clearly and lovingly. Our words have power, even as honey has healing properties, and our words carry the power of life.

Words spoken over us by ourselves or others are of great importance: they carry the power to hurt us or heal us, and they can cause us to doubt or to hope. Just as a king's decree was overturned by making another decree in Bible times, so the pain and sting of harmful, hurtful words is broken by speaking words of blessing and life.

Learning from The Bee

The name Deborah means "bee." The story of Deborah, found in Judges 4 and 5 in the Bible, is a story for our day. Though it is a story of a woman, it is also a story of and for men. (Women have been long been included in the Biblical term "sons of God," and men are part of the "bride of Christ.") As we delve into the life of this woman of God, we will discover that people like Deborah are desperately needed today. Anyone, man or woman, can be a Deborah.

By spending time in the Presence of the Lord, Deborah found a way to gather hope and wisdom to herself, and in a day when women were not educated or permitted to speak publicly, this brave lady listened to her Father and repeated what He said. The opportunity to express His heart presented itself again and again as men and women came to hear her words, and her declarations changed the course of a nation. The most unlikely of candidates, she became the leader of a great and mighty nation, leading a people back to the Father who loved them. Of all people, a *woman* used her voice to bring hope into dark days of terrorism and fear.

Despite great odds, Deborah found her voice and used it to speak the strategy of God to save her nation. She used her voice to effect change, and she put action to her words by being unafraid to do what she was asking of others: she went to battle against terror. I invite you to be like Deborah: find the heart of God for your family, city and nation, use your voice to speak the truth in love, take a stand for justice, and battle against terror with your voice. Deborah was desperately needed in her day: many like her are needed in our day, as well.

Seeds of Hope

I have to wonder: what set Deborah apart from the other women in her town? I understand the call of God, the gifts that He gave and her response to His call, but what amazes me is that Deborah took full advantage of the opportunity presented to her.

Deborah had to decide what she was going to do with what had been given to her. She had 24 hours in each of her days, just like everyone around her. How in the world did she find time to get alone with God and listen to His heart for the wisdom to address the disputes and interactions of her neighbors? We read that she sat under a palm tree to judge the nation; it's obvious that she sat in the presence of God in order to know what Israel should do. I guess we could say that she listened to God's heart in her prayer closet instead of the gossip at the village well.

Nurturing Hope

Our world is crying out for Deborahs to awake and arise! To take a stand and speak forth the wisdom and hope won by the cross and resurrection of Jesus Christ. To see our nations turn toward Him, once again, and be saved from our fear and terror.

We have a great opportunity at our fingertips, if we will but reach out and take it. With God's love in our hearts, His word in our hands and the hope for a great awakening to His presence, we as God's people can stand as gatekeepers at the entrance to our lives, guarding what comes in and what goes out of our families, our cities and our nations. I believe Holy Spirit is just waiting to be welcomed in so that God's Kingdom can grow as a mighty tree among us.

Father God is waiting for us to awaken and arise as Deborah did. He is eager for us to humble ourselves and listen to His heartbeat, to use the voice He's given us to change the earth's atmosphere from one of defeat and despair to one of victory and hope. As we declare His promises rather than the world's problems, we will see Psalm 24:7 become a reality: "Lift up your heads, oh you gates! And be lifted up, you everlasting doors, that the King of Glory shall come in." He wants to be invited to enter the gates of every life and family, every door of every city and nation, and His desire to dwell with us is our greatest hope!

Dear Lord, we, your people, humbly welcome you in.

TWO
Those Who Have Songs To Sing

God summons us into our potential.

Bill Johnson

Each of us has a story. Is it possible that each of us also has a song?

I read recently of a tribe in a remote part of Africa in which a woman, when she learns she is pregnant, goes off by herself for a few days until she "hears" her baby's song. The expectant mother then comes back to her village and teaches this song to the baby's father and all of the villagers, and when they are with the mother, they sing this song over the baby in utero. It's easy to imagine the mom singing or humming this tune throughout the day as she walks around and during the night when she lies awake, looking at the stars overhead. It's the song of her baby's life and destiny, full of hope and courage and strength.

When the baby is born, those in attendance sing the baby's song to welcome the child into the world. Throughout the child's life this song is sung, but only to him. No one else has the same song, and no one else ever will. It's the song for this child, and when the child dies — no matter how young or how old he is — the song is sung over the grave and then never sung again.

Somehow, the mothers in this remote African tribe know what some of us with lots of education missed: we each have a song. Our song is as unique and individual as we are. It is lovely and hopeful and filled with promise, just because it is ours and was given to us by our Heavenly Father.

What about you? Have you ever considered that there is a song that is uniquely yours, a song that only you can sing? Do you remember singing your own song as a child? Do you remember it still?

When the Music Stopped

I grew up in the coal mining region of western Pennsylvania. It is a beautiful place, and I was blessed with a family that gave me all the love they had in every way they knew how to give it. We were a church-going family, and if the doors were open, we were there, always sitting in the same pew. I remember not really liking the sermon times. How boring! But the songs — when we stood to sing hymns or the Doxology, I sometimes felt as though my spirit would soar right over those beautiful, wooded hills and take me with it. How could my feet stay on the ground when the Spirit of God was this close and this real?

Life was good and life was hard in our "valley between two hills." When I was two years old my mother died suddenly, leaving behind four children, the youngest of whom was only three days old. I can tell you that on that day my song changed forever. For years it seemed that I could only sing in a minor key. Laughter was common in our home, but deep happiness and the carefree joy of childhood seemed to have left on the day that Mom's song was last heard there. The good news and testimony of my life is that God is a healer and a redeemer. As I allowed Him to have His rightful place as Lord in my life, He was able to restore all that was lost – even my song.

It can be the same for you.

Looking for Love in all the Wrong Places

I loved Pennsylvania — I still do — and I remember feeling sorry for people who had to live somewhere else. I loved my family, and I grew up knowing that they loved me. I was active in the youth group and the choir at church, and I accepted Jesus into my life in second grade. Even so, I somehow never felt completely secure or at home. I wasn't at home in Pennsylvania among my classmates, in my church or even in my family that loved me. In fact, I wasn't at home in my own skin. The reason? I wasn't at home in love.

I knew that something was missing and drastically wrong, but I didn't know what it was or where to find it. I started looking for my identity — my song — in many of the places young people are wont to look, and surprise! It wasn't there. When I looked around me and played the comparison game that all women play, I realized what the problem was: I wasn't smart enough! I wasn't tall enough! I wasn't creative, spontaneous, organized or athletic enough! I needed to be kinder, gentler with my words, more thoughtful, send birthday cards on time, and stop sweating. I should pray more, give more, listen more and eat less. I needed to start exercising more, to begin wearing makeup and shaving my legs. "Now I think I've got it!" I said to myself. "Now I'll feel at home being me."

Guess what? It didn't work.

Hearing a Distant Tune

In 1980 I married Jim, the godliest man I know. "Wow," I thought, "someone like this loves me and married me! NOW I'll get my song back."

Guess what? It didn't work.

Jim and I were blessed with four amazing children. My heart's desire to be a wife and mother was now fulfilled, and I thought that I would be at peace inside myself. Now, surely I would know who I was and would be at home in my love for my family. Surely my song would flow effortlessly and with great beauty.

Guess what? That didn't work, either.

Jim went to Bible School, then planted and pastored a church. Believe me: for finding my worth and value and song, that really didn't work! By this time I was in my late 30's and was beginning to think that I would never really belong anywhere. No place felt like home, and I thought that maybe my song had died with my mom. Maybe I'd never really had a good song of my own.

Then came the call to southeast Asia.

Finding Myself in God's Heartbeat

In the late 90's Jim and I moved our family of six to a country in SE Asia. Many years before, by the time I was eight years old, I already had a deep-seated love for that faraway land. I had no idea my childhood fascination was part of the song I'd been given to sing.

Those Who Have Songs To Sing

I was invited to be an English teacher on a college campus there, a job for which I knew I was technically unqualified. Yet, the day I began my journey there and stood in front of my classes, my song suddenly came back to me! There it was! This is what I was created for, this is where I belonged!

Was this far away nation my real home? No. Rather, I had traveled halfway around the world to discover that my only true home was my Heavenly Father's love. There was no way I could do enough or change my looks enough to fit in. I was at home when I remembered His love for me and relaxed in His embrace. There in Asia, where I couldn't speak the language and didn't even know how to buy food, I began to understand that Papa, Father God, was enough for me. In a place where I felt totally vulnerable and unable to help myself, God's love was all the home I needed. As I stood in that foreign classroom, I knew I was unable to do what was asked of me on my own, but I also knew that I was not alone. I knew that my Father was not only pleased with me but was also encouraging me to sing the song He had placed in my heart long ago. Being at peace with Him and at rest in His love was what I had spent my whole life searching for.

You see, I have loved Jesus as long as I can remember. I don't remember ever not loving Him, so the problem with my song was not that I wasn't saved. I was. The problem was not that I didn't know love, but that I was not at home in love, and because I wasn't at home in love, I wasn't at home anywhere. I had to go to Asia to find my place of belonging and to understand what it means to be adopted as His fully loved daughter.

The great news is that we don't have to go to Asia or Africa or anywhere else to learn who we really are. Our songs are as close as our breath. Making our identities whole in God by learning to know Him is the key to discovering the songs we were given to sing.

Slowing Down to Remember

I am writing this in what God has intended as a season of rest. I'm finding rest to be a great concept but a difficult discipline. I'm not proud of the fact that true rest is a challenge for me, but I am glad that I'm finally learning the importance of obedience in this area.

If I were to ask any of the people I know what they have been doing lately, chances are that their responses would begin something like, "Oh, I've been so busy!" It's the catch phrase of our day. It defines us and gives us an excuse for almost anything that we haven't done or don't want to do. In our excessive busyness, our emotions sometimes get so cluttered and chaotic that "knowing we belong" gets lost in the shuffle, and we forget how secure we are in the Father's heart. Then we get even busier trying to fill the void that nothing can fill except God's love. We forget the song He sang over us when He knit us together in our mother's womb, and we start thinking that we must do something more to feel fulfilled. We tend to forget that He is longing to embrace us. He aches to enfold us in His arms and let us relax there, if we will stay still long enough.

As my children started going out with their friends during their teenage years (without parents along!), I always said to them as they left the house, "I love you. Have fun, be safe, and remember whose you are." They knew what that meant: "Remember that you carry the family name. It's an honorable name, and you are representing it when you walk out the door. Even more important, you carry the name of Jesus wherever you go. It's the Name above all Names and you represent it everywhere you go. Remember, because in remembering Who loves you and to Whom you belong, you will be wise when you choose your words and actions." Did it keep them from all harm and teenage adventure? No, but to this day they understand that remembering whose they are is a good way to follow their hearts and not to engage in whatever feels right at the time.

As we remember Who our Father God truly is, we are reminded of who and Whose we are. In those two realities alone we find great hope — hope — an expectation filled with confidence that the good we long for will be fulfilled.

Hope is found in His Presence

It only takes turning on the news for five minutes or glancing at the headlines of the day's newspaper to know that the world could use a tune-up. There's a lot to worry and fret about, and if there's one thing most of us do well, it's worry! When I get worried, I repeatedly find myself reading through Psalm 37, a psalm written by David to remind himself that the Lord is in control, not evil-doers. Verse 8 reads: "Cease from anger, and forsake wrath; Do no fret … it only causes harm."

Having grown up in Pennsylvania and married into life in Iowa, I have always loved clouds. One of my fondest childhood memories is lying on the ground with my siblings, ¬looking up at the clouds and imagining what we saw there. It's amazing how many chickens and spaceships and clown shoes a child can find in the shifting shape of a cloud!

Now that I live in California, I don't often see clouds in the summertime. The sun blazes hot and furious in the summer months, and temperatures often reach over 100 degrees Fahrenheit. Though I miss clouds, I know that the lack of them is part of the reason that crops grow so well here. Since sunshine is predictable day after day, crops are irrigated with the perfect amount of water to assure a bountiful harvest.

Unabated sunshine is also part of the reason that people travel here. Florida and Hawaii are great getaway spots for those who live through the bone-chilling winters of the northern states. It's good to have unclouded sunshine. It makes us feel healthy and free, unhindered by coats and boots and gloves. Its brightness can help chase away the blues, and some people linger in its heat and power for such long periods of time that they even look different with their newly acquired tans.

I want my relationship with Jesus to be that way. No clouds of shame or insecurity blocking my vision of His face. No veil of religion or hopelessness to prevent me from looking into His eyes of love. I want to linger in His warmth and presence until I am changed, looking more like Him.

When sin abounds in a nation, when it goes unchecked by righteousness and justice, it's as though God's face, His presence, can be eclipsed by clouds of fear, shame, worry and anger. If that happens, we don't see Him clearly. We begin to forget what He looks like and what His heart is like, and then both as individuals and nations we forget who we really are. We let go of "Whose we are;" we believe neither that He is good, nor that in His goodness He would want the likes of us.

The Sound of Victory

How many times God has shown Himself faithful in each of our lives? When was the last time you stopped to recapture the awe of His intervention in a situation you thought impenetrable? Have you taken time to thank Him for His graces, large and small, that we so easily take for granted? Have you dared to sing your own song to Him? From your heart, from the depths of who you are, just sing out that He is good. It's not about carrying a tune or making it rhyme. It is about having an attitude of worship and a grateful heart for who

He is. The sound of victory is not orchestrated or rehearsed; rather, it is a visceral response from the deep places within us that cry out to praise Him. It seems that the more honest and real our response to His love, the more symphonic it sounds to His ears, no matter how out of key our cries may be. It's time for us, His children, to wake up and sing to our Father once again. He'll never tire of hearing us remind Him how much we love and value knowing Him as Papa God.

Many years ago, while working in a remote area of central Asia, Jim and I were invited into a village of a people group that had been discovered just a few months previously. (For safety's sake, I will not name the village or the people group.) When we met with them to worship, I found it fascinating that the one thing one young woman most desired was the ability to sing her own song to the Lord. May her story that follows be the catalyst for you to sing your own song once again.

The Sound of His Coming

The noisy din of travelers told us that we were nearing the bus station long before it came into view. A cacophony of strange dialects rose above the piercing calls of street vendors, whose simple wooden carts were piled high with bananas or steamed buns which would put a few coins in their pockets and bring a bit of relief for the travelers' awakening hunger. Sunrise glistened off the dew that nighttime had sprinkled on the palm tree fronds, and red geraniums gleamed brightly along the cracked, uneven sidewalks. Soon the dew would be replaced with dust as the city stirred to a new day.

We piled into a crowded van and then rode past vibrant green rice paddies and fields of rape seed plants that waved their little yellow blossoms in the strengthening sunshine. Our destination was a village hidden high up in the rainforest. Upon arriving at the foot of the mountain, the driver's challenge was to create his own road. His only guide was a trail that had been engineered by daily tramping of water buffalo that had been led by their herders, year after routine year, between field and home.

Wide, shoeless feet kicked up dust as the villagers hurried out to greet us, and we soon banqueted together on rice and vegetables with the sense of being at a family reunion. After the simple, happy meal, we gathered on the rustic bamboo floor of our host's home, where Peter, a local teacher, shared from the Bible and led us in worship songs that he had painstakingly translated from English into the villagers' native tongue. We were miles from nowhere, yet we felt completely at home in the Kingdom of God, there on G___ Mountain.

During worship one young woman stepped out of her inherited shyness and asked me to pray for her. She explained that during the revolution, the government had thrown their indigenous drums and musical instruments into the river, forbidding them to sing their songs or dance in their traditional ways. After years of cultural oppression, their own sound and steps were long forgotten. Her request: for Holy Spirit's anointing to release the new sounds and steps through which He would receive glory from the G___ tribe.

With a sense of destiny being lived out, I laid my hands on this young revivalist's head and prayed that her cry would bring heaven to this earthen vessel and that she might pour out rivers of praise. And sure enough, as her voice and feet were quickened in response to His love, hope for a visitation of God's presence among her people was restored.

As late as the early 21st century, the world hadn't yet discovered the hidden beauty of the forgotten G___ people. When a team of missionary doctors discovered them, we were asked to pray for an open heaven and access to interact with them – not an easy task in this restricted-access nation. But the Spirit of God has no boundaries, so we began thanking Him for His strategy to reach them with His love. Within a few months, five young G___ women accepted the invitation to come into the city to learn simple medical procedures, such as hand washing and how to tend a wound. During those few weeks of training in an environment different from any they had experienced before, four of them met a Father they had never known, and they accepted the gift of Jesus.

There was a newfound respect afforded these "educated" women upon their return home. Their words now carried weight and authority, so when they shared their understanding of a God who is love, the seeds of life found heart soil that was tilled and fertile. Many in the G___ tribe soon became filled with the presence of the Lord, and knowledge of Him began to fill every place that had been low, broken and empty. There on the top of this dusty mountain, God's rain came, and a River began to flow.

In the years afterward, God's presence was expressed to the degree that the authorities became concerned and tried to stifle the G___ people again. But the unstoppable Kingdom is there, and when I think of the G___ people, I picture my sister, stepping a new way into the rice paddy, singing a new song over the seedlings as she plants and over the grain as she harvests, releasing the sound of heaven over the hidden beauty of the villages at the top of the mountain past the end of the road.

I believe that hope is one of the things that our present world longs for and needs most; finding and applying it is one of the many things we can learn from the life of Deborah.

The Expectation of Good

In the midst of all the clamor and frightening newscasts around us, it's very easy to lose our song and to forget that we belong in God's heart. We need to be reminded often of Whose we are. Hope is our portion from the Lord, and we will find hope for our days as we look together at the story of Deborah, which is found in Judges 4 and 5 of the Bible's Old Testament. Though I've never once heard a teaching or sermon on this passage, I believe it holds many keys to our successful navigation of the 21st century. The characters involved were unique, yet not so different from us, and they can help us discover how to live with great expectation of good – that is, with hope - in all circumstances of our lives.

Wake Up and Sing!

Deborah didn't just have a message, she lived a message. Before God gave her the military strategy to save her nation from the terror of a military siege, she learned how to sing her own song, how to believe fully in the potential of her destiny. Her interactions with her fellow Israelites and her devotion to God, her husband and her nation demonstrated to her countrymen what God was saying to them, of what His heart looked like toward them.

Just as Miriam and Moses each sang a song of victory following the Red Sea escape, Deborah sang a song of victory following Israel's rescue from the terror of King Jabin of Canaan. In verse 12 of chapter 5 of Judges we read, "Awake, awake, Deborah! Awake, awake, sing a song!" At this point the battle was already won, and the people were crying out for Deborah's voice to be lifted in a victory song. As her voice rang out through the atmosphere and over the land, all of creation knew the God of Israel was faithful. He was conqueror. He was righteous. Deborah's voice opened the heavens so that the sun of His presence was no longer clouded, and nothing hindered the Israelite's gaze as they recounted His righteous acts in song. There is great power in singing the praises of God!

THREE

Pursuing Destiny

*The real test of a man (or woman) is not when he plays
the role that he wants for himself,
but when he plays the role destiny has for him*

Vaclav Havel

The story of Deborah reads like a movie script, and though contained in only two chapters of the Book of Judges, the scenes and characters are so well depicted that they nearly spring to life from the page. The lives of two women, Deborah and Jael, are highlighted as they rout terrorism from their land. Barak, is the general of the Israeli army, and a terrorist named Sisera complete the list of main characters. Frankly, I'm shocked that it hasn't made the big screen yet.

Chapters 4 and 5 of Judges are usually called the story of Deborah, although a woman named Jael is also featured in the story. In a culture that neither honored nor educated women, both Deborah and Jael did some incredibly hard and brave things. Despite being considered second-class citizens, they had the confidence to do what needed to be done because they remembered Whose they were. Though they lived under an evil dictator's regime, they were not part of it. Deborah and Jael belonged to Father God and were part of His Kingdom, and they already knew what Jesus told His disciples many years later: "If you belonged to the world, it would love you as its own. As it is, you do not belong to the world, but I have chosen you out of the world" (John 15:19). So it was for Deborah and Jael. So it is for us.

The Bible is not just a record of history, but a living, breathing book that speaks to us today. Because we should always be able to relate Bible stories to our own lives, I encourage you to read the story of Deborah in its entirety. I'm going to comment on certain parts of it and I want you to ask God how the issues within them apply to your life, your family and the place where you live and work. Each of you will see something different because Holy Spirit will speak to your unique situation. Take whatever He shows you and pray to know what your response should be. As you ask the Lord how this story applies to you and take time to listen to His response, He will increase your hope. I remember reading somewhere that hope gives us the ability to absorb and endure our destiny, and I know that God longs for us to live in the hope that He offers.

Deborah's Story

One of the first things that stands out about Deborah is that she never asks for notoriety or fame. Rather, her life is given to knowing the heart of Father God.

To know a person's heart takes time and effort. Deep friendships and lasting marriages are formed on a foundation of slowing down and just being with loved ones – listening to their stories, hearing their opinions, understanding their fears and sharing their victories. Love naturally makes us want to spend as much time with another as possible, and when we're apart, we find ourselves wanting to share whatever we're doing and enjoying.

I believe that Deborah spent lots of time in the presence of God – not just telling Him what she wanted or thought, but obviously humbling herself in His holy presence to listen. Without hesitation or qualm, she used the wisdom and strategy of heaven to direct the army of Israel to go up against a terrorist organization. Knowing that the odds were against her nation, she was bold in the confidence and hope that she had heard heaven's perspective on how to battle Israel's foes. Deborah was seeking neither a name for herself nor fame that would go down through the ages; she was playing the role that the One she loved had given her. Love poured out from God into her heart, giving her hope that didn't disappoint. (See Romans 5:5.)

Judges, Chapters 4 and 5

The Book of Judges is a history of the Israelites, God's chosen people, spanning the time between Joshua's leadership and Israel's first monarchy when Saul was chosen as king. While the names may be strange to us and the particulars unique to this period in history, we can glean much from the events recounted there. It's amazing how much this story sounds like today!

Though the prophet Moses led the newly freed Israelites' exodus from Egypt, his disobedience prevented him from entering the Promised Land that they had traveled so long to possess, and Joshua was appointed as the leader who would take the people into

Canaan. (See Deuteronomy 32:48-52.) Following Joshua's death, "the Lord raised up judges, who saved them out of the hands of ... raiders" (MSG, Judges 2:16).

The Lord's desire was that the Israelites enter Canaan, occupy it, displace the Canaanites and cleanse the land of foreign, pagan gods. The Israelites, after centuries of slavery in Egypt and 40 years of wandering in the desert, would now have a land of their own in which they could rest. That was God's heart: He wanted a land and a people set apart for Himself, where the covenants given to Abraham would be fulfilled and the Kingdom of God would be displayed on earth. His people would serve Him and further His Kingdom in a land of milk and honey.

It is difficult if not impossible for us to imagine the paradigm shift that the nation of Israel underwent at that time. For centuries the Israelites had been brutally worked in the intense heat of the Egyptian sun. Day in and day out, their lives had been under the constant surveillance of their masters. Unrelenting hardships had become the norm of their existence. Coffee breaks, tea times and lunch hours were not a part of their schedule, nor did they go home at night to air conditioned houses and swimming pools. Hard work and pain were all they knew.

> *A bee is never as busy as it seems;*
> *it's just that it can't buzz any slower.*
>
> Kin Hubbard

So here was God, leading His people out of Egyptian slavery into a land of milk and honey where they could worship Him freely, and doing it with the express purpose of giving them rest. Rest! But like the bee who can't slow down its buzz, the Israelites' emotions and minds were always abuzz, and they couldn't slow down and live in the freedom they'd been given. Why? Scripture tells us they could not enter the promise of rest because of their unbelief:

> *"Who were they who heard and rebelled? Were they not all those Moses led out of Egypt? And with whom was he angry for forty years? Was it not with those who sinned, whose bodies perished in the wilderness? And to whom did God swear that they would never enter his rest if not to those who disobeyed? So we see that they were not able to enter, because of their unbelief."*
> NIV, Hebrews 3:16-19

> *"There remains therefore a rest for the people of God. Let us therefore be diligent to enter that rest ... for the Word of God is sharper than any two-edged sword, piercing even to the division of soul and spirit, and is a discerner of the thoughts and intentions of the heart."*
> Hebrews 4:9, 11-12

What a Father! What a Papa! What a heart of goodness that His call and desire are for His people to enter rest. Today, in a society that encourages and applauds "busyness" as a sign of importance and success, Papa God calls us to His perfect rest, just as He did the Israelites. Out of slavery, into sonship. At rest and peace in His presence. Wow.

So What Were Judges and Why Did Israel Need Them?

The Israelites often saw God come through for them in miraculous ways, yet they turned around and questioned His goodness the next time they were faced with difficulty. Having been miraculously freed

An Unclouded Sun

from a life of slavery, having walked through the wilderness without becoming ill or needing new clothes or shoes (I don't imagine there were many shopping malls in the Sinai in those days!), having eaten health food from heaven in the form of manna, still they doubted God's goodness and ongoing provision. And once in the Promised Land, they turned their eyes toward the foreign gods that were worshiped there. Instead of routing these gods from the land as God had intended, they allowed their hearts to follow the longing of their eyes, and soon they compromised and embraced false gods in place of the God of their father, Abraham.

The Israelites forgot Whose they were, and in forgetting their identity as God's chosen people, they settled in their new land by embracing the gods, social life, morals and religious beliefs and practices that they had been commissioned to displace. Though they saw themselves as free people, no longer in servitude to Pharaoh, they had exchanged their physical chains for those of a more insidious master: the gods of this world. Judges 17:6 describes this time: "In those days Israel had no king: everyone did as he saw fit." (NIV)

In the book of Judges we see Israel cycle through disobedience, which opened the door to the foreign oppression that caused them to cry out in distress. God, ever merciful, heard the cries of His children and sent a deliverer, in this case a judge, to help them in throw off the yoke of the enemy and lead them back into true freedom and rest.

The role of a judge included more than settling disputes. The Hebrew word for judge, "shofet," connotes judging, governing, passing down divine judgment, sentencing and making decisions in controversial situations, and the position entailed ruling in all judicial, legislative and military matters. During times of peace a judge settled disputes and problems in society; in times of war he organized the battle plans and rallied troops. The judges' rulership came from God, and because of this divine appointment, judges were the ultimate ruling authority over Israel. As executive, religious and military leaders, they were highly respected and honored as the ones to whom God had given the wisdom and ability to break political oppression and lead the nation back to the blessings of rest and peace.

God's Chastening Is His Mercy

Judges 4:1-2 tells us that "When Ehud was dead, the children of Israel again did evil in the sight of the Lord. So the Lord sold them into the hand of Jabin king of Canaan, who reigned in Hazor. The commander of his army was Sisera…".

Why would a good God "sell" His own people into Jabin's hand? Our God is also a God of justice, and He had made it very clear to the nation of Israel that obedience would bring abundant blessings and that disobedience would bring serious consequences. (Read Deuteronomy 28.) His plan was to keep the nation of Israel separated to Himself because out of her He would bring forth His Son. God loved His people so much that He could not look the other way when they strayed from His laws, and as Proverbs 13:24 tells us, "He who spares his rod hates his son, But he who loves him disciplines him promptly."

God was not treating the Israelites as slaves but as sons. Look at Hebrews 12:5-6:

And you have forgotten the exhortation which speaks to you as to sons: My son, do not despise the chastening of the Lord, nor be discouraged when you are rebuked by Him. For whom the Lord loves He chastens, and scourges every son whom He receives.

Revelation 3:19 admonishes us that as many as God loves, He chastens. What does the word "chasten" mean? According to Strong's Exhaustive Concordance, the Hebrew meaning is "to give reproof, warning or instruction, restraint and discipline" (4148). The Greek meaning is "to train up a child, to educate by discipline, to instruct, to learn or to teach" (3811). God's chastening, discipline, and instruction are His way of protecting His covenant people and bringing them back into right relationship with Him. In essence, He chastens His people to remind them Whose they are. In Israel's case, not only was He faithful to the covenant He made with Abraham to bless and keep His people, but He was also faithful to keep His covenant described in Leviticus and Deuteronomy which spelled out the curses that would come with disobedience.

The Right Side of the Road

It's unfortunate that discipline has come to have such a negative connotation. I understand that many people cringe at the thought of discipline because they have experienced abuse, but abuse and true discipline are two totally different things. As with most things, I have a simplified way of looking at this: I liken God's discipline to parenting.

It's my belief that parents who don't spend much time in prayer change their ways in a hurry when their children start to drive! Just the thought of teenagers behind the wheel of a car strikes terror into parents everywhere. The new freedom of driving comes at a time when many young people are ready to express their independence and are not always eager to listen to Mom and Dad's words of caution.

I remember teaching (by definition, disciplining) my children as they were getting ready to leave the house. I told them that technically they could drive down whichever side of the road they wanted to. Imagine the shocked looks I got! I went on to explain that since their dad and I wouldn't be in the car, there was nothing we could do if they decided that driving down the wrong side of the highway would be a thrill. I went on to explain that if they did so, however, the results would likely be immediate and drastic: either a head-on collision with who knows what or a friendly state trooper to remind them of what was right. I was explaining to my children that the rules of the road were not designed to punish them but to keep them safe. Those yellow and white lines were not painted on the tarmac to keep them from having fun but to protect them. So, while technically they could drive on either side of the road, their dad and I recommended staying to the right.

The laws and boundaries of love that God has given to us in His word are similar. He didn't put them there to punish us or keep us from enjoying life, but to keep us safe from perils that we can't see around the next bend. And when we choose to break the law, our actions cause a reaction – either the discipline of our Papa or a head-on collision with sin and the resultant pain. As children of God, we are wise to choose discipline given in love.

Consequences of Forgetting

Let's read the first few lines of Judges 4 again.

When Ehud was dead, the children of Israel again did evil in the sight of the LORD. So the LORD sold them into the hand of Jabin king of Canaan, who reigned in Hazor. The commander of his army was Sisera, who dwelt in Harosheth Hagoyim. And the children of Israel cried out to the LORD; for Jabin had nine hundred chariots of iron, and for twenty

An Unclouded Sun

years he had harshly oppressed the children of Israel.

Judges 4:1-3

"Did evil" is defined here as the Israelites forgetting their covenant with God and worshiping the idols of the people around them. Do we have idols in our lives today? I heard someone say in a sermon once that an idol is anything you have to check with before you say yes to God.

The following scripture is part of the song that Deborah sang after the victory over Sisera:

In the days of Shamgar son of Anath, in the days of Jael, the roads were abandoned; travelers took to winding paths. Village life ceased until I, Deborah, arose, arose a mother in Israel. When they chose new gods, war came to the city gates, and not a shield or spear was seen among forty thousand in Israel.

Judges 5:6-8

In Deborah's song we learn why there was an enemy loose in the land: "they chose new gods." The consequences of idolatry were serious. Roads were empty of both commercial and everyday traffic because people were afraid to travel, and when they did choose to go out, they were so terrorized that they looked for secret, back roads on which they might slip by the enemy unnoticed.

Another huge problem was the imbalance of weaponry; there was no standing army in Israel at this time. When a judge called for an army to rally, it was up to the common people to volunteer, much like the Minuteman Militia in the early days of our own nation. How dire their situation was! What hope could they possibly have when the odds were stacked so high against them? How could they fight a heavily armed enemy when they were forbidden to have weapons and were too afraid to go outside their homes? Such was the situation in which the Israelites found themselves.

Finding Hope

It's not so different in many places today. Details may vary, but fear is fear and oppression is oppression. Here in the United States we might not be afraid to walk down our country roads or go about daily life, but we can get caught up in the confusion and terror of the age. Whichever enemy we are facing in our life — sickness, financial setbacks, broken relationships, family members making destructive choices, or the constant menu of fear served up by the media — it is easy to view our enemy as bigger, stronger and better equipped than we are. We see our children and our future at risk, and we wonder what it will take to win in the face of such overwhelming odds.

We aren't given much description of Deborah: "Now Deborah, a prophetess, the wife of Lappidoth, was judging Israel at that time." (Judges 4:4). We shouldn't be surprised that the Word of God doesn't describe her physical features, her education level, or her financial position, because what we view as qualification for success is not what God takes into account. The Bible says in 1 Samuel 16:7 that God looks not on outward appearance but on the heart. Phew! Aren't you grateful that He puts within us the very gifts and anointing that He wants to manifest through us? It's not about our age or size, whether we are male or female, wealthy or highly educated. Being used by God is a matter of our availability and His grace.

Here is what we do know about Deborah. She is the fourth of twelve judges named in the Book of Judges. She is also the only judge called a prophet before the time of Samuel. She is identified as the wife of Lappidoth. She led Israel, and the people of Israel came to her for settlement of their disputes. Deborah broke free of cultural restrictions and expectations to become all she was created to be. At a time when hopelessness permeated the society around her, she tuned her ear toward the good news of hope and restoration that resonated from God's heart. She was courageous in matters of state and knew her countrymen well. I like to think of it this way: Deborah knew Whose she was. She was aware that she wasn't merely a number in an obscure ledger in God's heavenly library. Rather, she knew that she was His well-loved daughter who could come to Him, listen to His heartbeat and sing its hopeful rhythm to her fellow Israelites, who lived in fear of the next terrorists' attack.

Deborah had a weapon that we need to lay hold of and sharpen today – the weapon of hope. Deborah understood the seriousness of her nation's situation, and she was able to access hope from heaven, then agree with that hope and use it as a weapon against fear and discouragement.

What terrorizes you, today? Loneliness, illness, financial trouble, sin, shame, memories, regrets? Be a Deborah! Remember Whose you are! Spend time with the Father and allow Him to encourage you with hope.

FOUR

Named With Purpose And Hope

A good name is rather to be chosen than great riches...

Proverbs 22:1

Deborah's story fascinates me. I have read it many times over the years, and each time it basically said the same thing to me. I have learned, though, that because the Bible is the active and living Word of God, it contains layers of revelation just waiting to be discovered by those who love Him. As my pastor Bill Johnson says, God doesn't hide things from us, but for us, so I knew there had to be more. I began asking God to reveal secrets hidden in the story.

I've always liked words – the sound of them, the feel of them, the impact and power of them. Even the mysterious power of their spoken inflection fascinates me, so when I started searching for deeper meaning in the story of Deborah, I became intrigued by many of the words – words I could not pronounce and did not understand. Many of them were names of the characters and locations in the story, and being unfamiliar with the nation of Israel and the Hebrew language, I began digging around to find out if these names were significant. I soon discovered that God didn't waste any words when He inspired the writing of His book. In fact, this already marvelous story becomes even more dynamic when we understand the "rest of the story," hidden in the meaning of names.

Behind the Names

Deborah's name means bee. (Strong's Exhaustive Concordance, 1483) Most of us know that bees live in a perfectly ordered society inside their beehive, which suggests that Deborah's approach to life was organized. But the meaning of the root word from which her name comes is "to answer, declare or speak," which identifies Deborah as one who is called to speak the word of the Lord to Israel, calling the nation back to God.

Deborah's husband was Lappidoth, a name which means burning torch, lamp or flame. In scripture, a burning, blazing fire often represents the Presence of God. Symbolically, then, the names Deborah and Lappidoth represent a covenant relationship (marriage) between declaration and the presence of God's Holy Spirit.

Deborah spent time with the Lord, listening to His heart, learning His ways. As a prophetess, she declared the word of God, which means she took time to hear that word before speaking it. Psalm 119:103 reads, "How sweet are Your words to my taste, sweeter than honey to my mouth!" There in the secret place of prayer and worship, Deborah heard the words that the Lord was speaking to her. They gave her clarity and strong resolve in war, and they became as honey on her lips when she declared them to the children of Israel.

In verse 5 of chapter 4 we read that Deborah "...would sit under the palm tree of Deborah between Ramah and Bethel in the mountains of Ephraim. And the children of Israel came up to her for judgment". In fact, the palm tree was associated with her name and called The Palm of Deborah. Here, too, we find revelation: palm trees symbolically represent blessing and prosperity, both of which Deborah brought to the nation. The tree's location was between Ramah, which infers idolatry, and Beth-el, which means "house of Almighty God."

My friend Pat Tenant writes, "Deborah is meeting with and responding with supernatural wisdom to those seeking answers to the moral condition (lost) they are in. Symbolically I don't think you could paint a clearer picture of the 'bride of Christ,' the church, functioning as it should in a fallen world." If, in fact, Deborah can represent the Bride of Christ, the church, where in the story do we find the Bridegroom represented? If he is there, then this story of honor, relationship and freedom is also a type for us of the hope the church has of victorious partnership with Jesus.

> *"[Deborah] sent for Barak son of Abinoam from Kedesh in Naphtali and said to him, The Lord, the God of Israel, commands you: "Go, take with you ten thousand men of Naphtali and Zebulun and lead the way to Mt. Tabor. I will lure Sisera, the commander of Jabin's army, with his chariots and his troops to the Kishon River and give him into your hands."*
>
> NIV, Judges 4:6, 7

The name Barak means "lightning" or "flashing sword" (New Strong's Exhaustive Concordance, 1301). And what are we told about him? Who his daddy is. The Bible makes it clear that it's important to know and remember Whose we are. Barak's father is named Abinoam, which translates "father of pleasantness, grace, delightfulness and splendor," who lives in Kedesh, "sanctuary of holiness." What a clear picture of Jesus, the Bridegroom and Father God!

Deborah gave Barak the word of the Lord: she prophesied to him that he was to deploy troops and go into battle, so we can assume that he was a commander in Israel's volunteer army. He was to take dominion over the land and redeem it from foreign domination, which is a symbolic picture of what Christ accomplished through His finished work on the cross. According to Mark 16:15-18 and Matthew 28:18-20 it is also one of the commissions Jesus gave His people, the church, here on earth.

War Strategies

Not one to pull any punches, Deborah told Barak straight out that God would deploy Sisera (the bin Laden of his day) against him and would deliver Sisera into Barak's hand. In the natural way of thinking, this made no sense at all. Barak was being told to lead a division of 10,000 soldiers without artillery against the tyrant, Sisera, whose name means "hawk eye" and whose army was equipped with 900 chariots of iron. These were not chariots designed for a family outing by the Red Sea; they were war tanks, equipped with large knives on the wheels, designed to cut down everyone and everything that got close. Israel had only primitive weapons such as farm implements and household items. The odds were in favor of the army with tanks, not the one with pitchforks and frying pans. In our day, we might compare a battle between the Israelite volunteers and Sisera's troops to hand-to-hand combatants against tanks, so when Israel was victorious, it was an obvious show of divine help:

tactical strategies from heaven and direct favor from God in battle, both gained by Deborah in her time spent with God.

Confidence and Hope

Wow, what confidence Deborah had in her ability to hear God's voice! This bee, this spirited, fiery woman, chose her best general to do the impossible. She was willing to risk many lives, including her own, and she never stumbled with excuses or "what if's." And what confidence Barak had in Deborah's ability to hear God, as well! He, too, was willing to lead the troops into what would surely be a blood bath for Israel if they forgot Whose they were.

How about you? Are you Papa God's child? Do you know your Heavenly Father's voice? When things are scary and going wrong do you run to Him or from Him? We all belong in His heart and He is speaking; we, too, will hear what to do and how to do it if we will just lean on Him and listen. We can learn the strategies of heaven for fighting the good fight of faith here on earth — pulling heaven to earth, bringing the kingdom now, in our day, not waiting for some future time or people to do it, breaking free of terror and oppression and living in the freedom that Jesus already paid for.

He Knows My Name

I once heard Bill Johnson say that our purpose comes from being named by God. What hope that gives me! God knows my name. I'm not a ledger entry or a serial number; I am God's daughter, and He is acquainted with me. I am a member of His church and a part of His Bride — He loves me and gave His life for me.

God doesn't just tolerate us; He loves us. He values us. He accepts us. He chooses us. And He has named us. In other words, the divine Authority of all creation believes in us, and it would be foolish for us to waste His favor. My friend Anne Kalvestrand, director of *The Art of Peace Institute*, says that we don't need to fear failure. When we know we are protected and loved, we can dare to walk on water.

One of the burdens of visionary leaders is getting people to follow what they clearly see. Deborah knew her people well, both their strengths and their weaknesses. She believed in their ability to succeed at God's plan even though they were afraid. Because she loved God and her countrymen, the people recognized her authority and followed her prophetic voice. Because she knew how God saw her and was confident in her identity in Him, her leadership was effective and decisive.

Under the heading "Planning an Attack: Uniting Against Terror," author Gary Gagliardi translates the ancient wisdom of Sun Tzu's *The Art of War and Strategy Against Terror*:

> *We say: "Know yourself and know your enemy. You will be safe in every battle. You may know yourself but not know the enemy. You will then lose one battle for every one you win. You may not know yourself or the enemy. You will then lose every battle." (p 48)*

Deborah not only knew herself and her enemy, but she also knew her God. To know Him is to gain wisdom that we all can live by.

What Does Hope Look Like?

When the outcome of a given situation is obvious and the conclusion of a matter forgone, it doesn't take much to hope. All we have to do is allow our minds and emotions to flow with what is coming and then join in, "hoping" that all will turn out as planned.

Named With Purpose and Hope

But hope doesn't always make sense. What about the times when there just "ain't no way," when things don't look the way we thought they would or should? How do we find hope to sustain us in those times?

Hope doesn't have to make sense. It is at the most desperate and unlikely times that hope shines the brightest. When we hope against all reason, we display what it looks like to have a father, what it's like to be a daughter or a son.

You see, fathers give us our identity. A good father identifies what is wonderful in his children and then declares it over them. If your father sees kindness in you and tells you how kind you are, he has just named you Kind. Your dreams and potential are now limitless in the realm of kindness.

Fathers protect us, too, not only from our childhood fears and insecurities, but from living our lives in darkness, without boundaries or discipline. Good fathers turn on the light of Truth for us and paint "lines on the highway" so we know which way to go.

Fathers also leave us an inheritance. Proverbs 13:22 says, "a good father leaves an inheritance to his children's children."(NIV) Many people receive the blessings of financial inheritance or gifts of land and investments from their fathers, which is right and good. Even if your father didn't bestow you with financial gain, he was a good man if he raised you in truth, if he gave you a proper, healthy understanding of your identity and if he protected you by sharing Jesus with you. Inheritance comes in many forms.

Hope comes and hope is renewed when we embrace being adopted by Papa God. We no longer need fear what we don't know about the future, because Jesus knows, and we know Him. If you didn't have a father who gave you identity, protection or an inheritance, it's not too late. In the Bible, Father God has sent out the written decree of His desire that you be His child. Come out of your slavery and into His sonship by accepting His offer of eternal life through Jesus, the Son.

Father Abraham and Mother Sarah

Isn't it interesting that Father God would use the father of the Hebrew nation, Abraham, to show us how to hope? I don't know where Deborah found hope for better days for her nation other than in her time spent with the Father, the best place for all of us to recharge our hope. It wouldn't surprise me, though, if she recounted the testimony of Abraham and Sarah's longing for a child to encourage herself in the Lord.

Talk about a situation that didn't look like anyone thought it should! Abraham, having followed God faithfully, kept watching the days and years go by as he waited for the fulfillment of God's promise to give him a son. It's one thing to wait for a letter of recommendation or a check in the mail; it's another to wait for something that becomes more impossible with each passing day. Some of you know what I'm talking about because you've waited a long time to see your prayers answered. Perhaps you are waiting still. Grab hold of the lessons of Abraham's life for yourself.

It's All About a Faithful Father

I believe that Abraham could hold onto hope because he remembered his covenant with God. Abraham and Sarah were a man and a woman as we all are, yet they held on to God's promise when each shadow of the sundial seemed to push it further from reality. I want to know about and tap into that level of hope.

I love the way the Message Bible recounts the passages about Abraham:

"If Abraham, by what he did for God, got God to approve him, he could certainly have taken credit for it. But the story we're given is a God-story, not an Abraham-story. What we read in Scripture is, "Abraham entered into what God was doing for him, and that was the turning point. He trusted God to set him right instead of trying to be right on his own."
MSG, Romans 4:1a-3

A few months ago Jim and I took a road trip to Colorado from our home in northern California. It was wintertime, and during the first part of our trip, the scenery with the sun shining off fresh snow was stunning. Then we hit Salt Lake City, which, that day was a basin of fog. Driving mile after mile along the salt flats, the only colors in the landscape were white and gray. Even the highway was gray with dirty white and cowardly yellow lines. The Great Salt Lake was hidden by fog, as were most of the surrounding mountains. As the passenger in the car, I took time to journal my thoughts concerning what I was seeing out the window:

The world outside is indistinguishable. Mountains surround us on all sides, as do fields of snow-covered salt.

Low, gray clouds hug the squat, gray hills. A thin blanket of snow covers the barrenness of both the hillsides and the miles of dirty, gray salt.

Bleak. Nondescript. That's all I see.

Barren but for a few patches of brown weeds and a handful of stumpy, rugged trees. The trees, though seemingly dead, are still standing. Waiting, longing, hopeful for spring rain and sun.

A gray salt factory is tucked up against the mountains, spewing gray steam. Nothing, no color, no life stands out here today. This is what hopelessness is and feels like.

And suddenly I think of Sarah's womb. Barren, lifeless, hopeless. Then God shows up and says He will use that very womb as home to the promised child she and Abraham have waited for all these years.

I look at the world outside my car window and wonder what Jim's and my response would be if God told us to buy five acres here and plant corn? Or cabbages? Or anything at all? What if He said that all we've hoped and longed and prayed for would come to be through the crop we plant in a salt field? Would we do it? Invest the money, time and hope in land and seed and equipment, knowing the prospect is ludicrous from our human standpoint?

And now I understand why Sarah laughed when God said she would soon conceive. I'm trying to learn how she and Abraham hoped. It certainly was against all reason and hope. Yet, he believed God. And each month, each year, each decade, he knew, today might be the day.

I'm so glad it was a God-story and not an Abraham-story, that the outcome was based on what God did and not on what Abraham or Sarah did.

And therefore I, too, can hope. Against all reason and in the middle of a salt field, against all hope I do believe that God will do all He has said. Thanks, Abraham. Thanks, Sarah. Thanks, Papa.

Free to Hope

"O happy day, when Jesus washed my sins away." (Hawkins, Edwin. Oh Happy Day; lyrics)

The words of this song remind me that what I have to be grateful for so far outweighs what I have not yet received! This basic truth — that Jesus washed away my sin, so it's a happy day — has undone my yoke of doubt, disappointment and hope deferred.

Realizing that God our Heavenly Father has adopted us and given us a name filled with destiny, we can cling to hope in the midst of our bleakest days. He changed Abram's name to Abraham, "Father of Nations," long before Abraham fathered even one child. May this scripture from Psalm 119 be our cry as we live our lives with purpose and hope:

> *"I'm homesick- longing for Your salvation.*
>
> *I'm waiting for your word of hope.*
>
> *What you say goes, God, and stays, as permanent as the heavens.*
>
> *Your truth never goes out of fashion; it's as up-to-date as the earth when the sun comes up.*
>
> *Your Word and truth are as dependable as ever; that's what you ordered – you set the earth going.*
>
> *If your revelation hadn't delighted me so, I would have given up when the hard times came.*
>
> *But I'll never forget the advice you gave me; you saved my life with those wise words.*
>
> *Save me! I'm all yours. I look high and low for your words of wisdom.*
>
> *The wicked lie in ambush to destroy me, but I'm only concerned with your plans for me.*
>
> *I see the limits to everything human, but the horizons can't contain your commands!"*
>
> MSG, Psalms 119:81; 89-96

FIVE

Against All Odds

You can't afford to give Hitler Poland.

Susan Forward

Backing up a bit in the story, I want us to look at the passage in which Barak says he will go to battle against Sisera if Deborah will.

> And Barak said to Deborah, "If you will go with me, then I will go; but if you will not go with me, I will not go!" So she said, "I will surely go with you, nevertheless there will be no glory for you in the journey you are taking, for the Lord will sell Sisera into the hand of a woman." Then Deborah arose and went with Barak to Kedesh.
>
> Judges 4:8, 9

The strength of Deborah's confidence, the courage her presence inspired and her ability to hear the "now" word of the Lord on the battlefield all served Barak well. He knew she could be trusted; he would have known people who had gone to her for judgment and counsel — perhaps he, himself had. He knew that she heard the Father's voice. Perhaps he also wanted to release her into her call and destiny. In a male-dominated society, it's possible that he knew she needed him for permission to become who God created her to be.

Do you know people like Deborah? Don't you just feel safer when they are around? Where do they get that kind of courage? I believe that Deborah got hers by remembering Whose she was. She knew it wasn't about her or her ability to do, hear and say all the right things. I'm convinced that, with so many lives on the line, Deborah was certain that she belonged in the Father's heart. She knew He would not let her down, but rather would give her His strategy for the battle. After all, He had a much better view of the battlefield. Deborah didn't dare think about how inadequate she was, how outmanned and under-equipped the army of Israel was, or about what other people would think. She had to keep her mind fixed on the character of her Commander In Chief, on what He said He would do, and on what He had asked of her. Note that she didn't take on the burden of worrying about how to feed the army or where they would sleep – those concerns were for someone else to handle. Likewise, we are to focus on what He has asked of us and trust that others will handle the role they have been given.

Deborah had to remember to Whom she belonged, and in our day-to-day lives, so must we! We don't need to fear what we don't understand or know. Jesus understands and knows everything, and we know Him. The Man who is Truth delights in sharing what He knows with us.

Against All Odds

God Set the Trap

Deborah instructed Barak to head his troops to the river Kishon, and she told him that God would deploy Sisera, Jabin's commanding officer, and his troops there. The name Kishon means place of catch, and comes from a root word meaning to lay *bait or lure.*[1]

> *Barak called the tribes of Zebulun and Naphtali to Kedesh; he went up with 10,000 men under his command and Deborah went up with him.*
>
> *Now Heber the Kenite, of the children of Hobab the father-in-law of Moses, had separated himself from the Kenites and pitched his tent near the terebinth tree at Zaanaim, which is beside Kedesh.*
>
> Judges 4:10, 11

Barak did as instructed by the Lord through Deborah. He took his troops to Kedesh in Galilee, which means *sacred place,*[2] between what is today Lebanon and the Golan Heights. At first read, it seems odd that the Word switches from describing this battle preparation to mentioning a distant relative of Moses named Hobab, who was a nomad. We learn from this verse that Hobab lived separated from the rest of the Kenites, and we later discover that he was on good terms with the Canaanites. This is a foreshadowing of the trap that is being set for Israel's enemy.

A Different Perspective

The teaching I've heard on this discussion between Deborah and Barak has always been a bit clouded for me. Usually, the point

---

[1] "Meaning and Etymology of Biblical Names;" Abarim-Publications.com, accessed November 15, 2011

[2] Ibid.

made is that Barak is a huge wimp. How else could one explain his unwillingness to go to battle without Deborah?

This postulation doesn't make sense to me. I shudder to think that any man in any army could gain the position of authority over a nation's troops that Barak had and then be afraid to go to war without a woman at his side! Even the argument that he didn't want to go without her because of her prophetic insight only carries a certain amount of weight. The rank of general isn't extended to a man who is intimidated by battle, and it's unlikely that Barak would have refused to obey an order unless accompanied by the commander outranking him.

So how else can we explain Barak's request while staying inside the legal parameters of the Biblical script? Our answer could lie in Deborah's reply to Barak: she told him that she would go with him, but that he would not receive the glory for the victory. Rather, a woman would be given credit for Sisera's demise.

While the Bible doesn't tell us how Barak responded to this, the next thing we read is that Barak "went up with 10,000 men under his command and Deborah went up with him"(NIV, Judges 4:9,10). Instead of being put off or angry at the thought of a woman getting the glory for a battle he would lead and win, it seems as though he was okay with the idea. Perhaps it was even his idea all along.

A Picture of New Testament Reality

In John 14:12 Jesus tells us that we, the church, will do greater things than He did. Praying to His Father in Heaven about us (His church, the Bride), Jesus says, "I pray for them. I do not pray for the world but for those You have given me, for they are Yours. And all Mine are Yours, and Yours are Mine, and I am glorified in them" (NIV, John 17:9, 10). As we represent Jesus on the earth, He is glorified through our lives.

Using this understanding to look at the story of Barak and Deborah going to battle, we can view Barak and Deborah as a representation of Christ and His church. It is as if a prophetic picture is being painted for us. In it we see a strong, mighty commander who wants a woman to receive glory for the deeds they accomplish together: the Bridegroom receiving glory for the victories won by His bride.

This also makes sense in light of the concept that Barak wanted Deborah's prophetic insight on the field of battle. They didn't go to war thinking about Plan B in case they lost. They entertained no thought of losing. If God was calling them to battle, then victory was their portion.

A Complete Prophetic Picture

Because they give us insight, I am inserting the meanings of names in parentheses after they appear in the passage that recounts the battle:[3]

> *Deborah got ready and went with Barak (flashing sword) to Kedesh (consecrated or holy place). Barak called Zebulun and Naphtali together at Kedesh. Ten companies of men followed him. And Deborah was with him.*
>
> *It happened that Heber (to be joined with) the Kenite (wandering smith; metalworker) had parted company with the other Kenites, the descendants of Hobab, Moses' in-law. He was now living at Zaanammim Oak near Kedesh. They told Sisera (Hawk Eye is the closest translation, but is of uncertain origin) that Barak son of Abinoam had gone up*

---

[3] "Meaning and Etymology of Biblical Names;" Abarim-Publications.com, accessed November 15, 2011

to Mount Tabor. Sisera immediately called up all his chariots to the Kishon (to set a snare or lay a trap) River — nine hundred iron chariots! — along with all his troops who were with him at Harosheth Haggoyim.

Deborah said to Barak, "Charge! This very day God has given you victory over Sisera. Isn't God marching before you?"

Barak charged down the slopes of Mount Tabor, his ten companies following him.

God routed Sisera — all those chariots, all those troops! — before Barak. Sisera jumped out of his chariot and ran. Barak chased the chariots and troops all the way to Harosheth Haggoyim. Sisera's entire fighting force was killed — not one man left.

MSG, Judges 4:10-16

With Friends Like These

Sisera, the sole survivor of the Canaanite fighting machine, ran for cover. His army was defeated, and rather than terrorizing the local population, he was now being hunted and pursued. He apparently ran to the countryside in an effort to find a place to hide, because we read that he ended up at the tent of Heber the Kenite. (I'm assuming it was the countryside as the Kenites were nomads.)

Heber the Kenite was a nomadic metalworker. Some sources think that he worked in copper, others suggest iron. Either way, it seems to me that part of the reason he was friendly with Sisera could have been that Heber helped make the chariots and implements of war for Jabin's army. That's speculation on my part, but we know he wasn't making weapons for the Israelites, because the Word tells us that they had none. If Heber was indeed supplying the Canaanite forces with weapons of mass destruction, it makes the scenario that follows that much more ironic.

The Tent of Jael

In Judges 4:17 we read that there was peace between the home of Sisera's king, Jabin, and the home of Heber and Jael. It was no surprise that Sisera ran there, because he would have considered their home a safe house. There he was, the terrorist on the run, so a safe place to run was to the home of his weapons supplier, right?

I don't know if Jael was watching and waiting for Sisera and then invited him in, or if he knocked on the tent flap. (Is that even possible?) Either way, she invited him in, and she told him not to be afraid. She offered him rest and covered him with a blanket. (Be cautious when someone who is a friend by force tells you "I've got you covered!") He asked for a drink of water, and she gave him milk. What does a cup of milk do to a person who is exhausted? Makes them sleep. So far, it appears that Jael was doing all she could to protect and comfort the man who had brought terror to so many.

Sisera then instructed her to guard him and hide him:

And he [Sisera] said to her [Jael], "Stand at the door of the tent, and if any man come and inquires of you," and says, "Is there any man here?" you shall say, "No."
NIV, Judges 4:20

Sometimes what isn't recorded is as interesting as what is. Here we see Sisera telling Jael what she is to do, but there is no record of her response. Whether she didn't respond to Sisera's command or

Holy Spirit didn't include it because He knew we'd soon find out what she thought of it, the point is that she did not agree to hide him.

Ouch

The climax of the story is the fulfillment of Deborah's prophecy that Sisera would be given into the hand of a woman.

> *Then Jael, Heber's wife, took a tent peg and took a hammer in her hand, and went softly to him [Sisera] and drove the peg into his temple, and it went down into the ground; for he was fast asleep and weary. So he died. And then, as Barak pursued Sisera, Jael came out to meet him, and said to him, "Come, I will show you the man whom you seek." And when he went into her tent, there lay Sisera, dead with the peg in his temple.*
>
> NIV, Judges 4:21, 22

Jael, Heber's wife, took a tent peg in one hand and a hammer in the other, and soon had Israel's enemy nailed down. How could she commit such a gruesome act? Though she was not an Israelite by birth and her household had peace with Jabin, she surely must have experienced the tension of life under this evil and unpredictable tyrant. Like Deborah, she could stand by in fear of the enemy sleeping in her tent, or she could consider him as being given into her hand.

Just Doing What Comes Naturally

Jael was a nomad and the wife of a nomad, and she lived in a tent. What are nomads best known for? Moving. In the culture of Old Testament times, nomadic women wove the tent fabric, stitched the tents together, made the ropes to secure them, took the tents down and put them up when the family moved to greener pastures. For years, perhaps for most of her life, Jael had been using a hammer and tent pegs to secure the family dwelling in place. More than once this woman had stretched out her tent curtains, lengthened her cords and driven her tent pegs firmly into the ground.

You see, the Lord didn't require Jael to do something that she had no idea how to do. He used what was in her hand to defeat the enemy and bring peace to His people for the next 40 years.

And the word of the Lord saying that the enemy of God's people would be given into the hand of a woman was proven true. Deborah had received the tactical strategy from heaven, and Jael used the practical strategy of her everyday life. Both received glory for their part in defeating the enemy, and once again we see the heart of God displayed in His desire that each member of The Body fulfill its part in bringing glory to the Head, which is Christ.

> *For in fact the body is not one member but many. If the foot should say, "Because I am not a hand, I am not of the body," is it therefore not of the body? And if the ear should say, "Because I am not an eye, I am not of the body," is it therefore not of the body? If the whole body were an eye, where would be the hearing? If the whole were hearing, where would be the smelling? But now God has set the members, each one of them, in the body just as He pleased. And if they were all one member, where would the body be?*
>
> *But now indeed there are many members, yet one body. And the eye cannot say to the hand, "I have no need of you"; nor again the head to the feet, "I have no need of you." No, much rather, those members of the body which*

seem to be weaker are necessary. And those members of the body which we think to be less honorable, on these we bestow greater honor; and our unpresentable parts have greater modesty, but our presentable parts have no need. But God composed the body, having given greater honor to that part which lacks it, that there should be no schism in the body, but that the members should have the same care for one another. And if one member suffers, all the members suffer with it; or if one member is honored, all the members rejoice with it.

Now you are the body of Christ, and members individually.
1 Corinthians 12:14-27

Imagine — each part of the body working as it was designed to work, not trying to be another part or competing against another's gift, but functioning at full capacity in the way that only it can!

The Completed Bride

The story of Sisera's defeat is also a picture of the completed Bride of Christ — a picture of the time when Jew and Gentile will work together to take dominion. Barak was pleased and grateful that the women were praised. We know that he even joined in the celebration of them, because all of Judges 5 is a song that Deborah and Barak sang together — a song full of praises for these women and for this man, who together defeated terrorism and turned their land back to God. What a beautiful prophetic picture: The Bridegroom and the Bride, Jesus and His Church, completing, favoring and honoring one another as they defeat the enemy together and bring the Father praise:

Then Deborah and Barak the son of Abinoam sang on that day, saying:

When leaders lead in Israel,
When the people willingly offer themselves,
Bless the LORD!

Hear, O kings! Give ear, O princes!
I, even I, will sing to the LORD;
I will sing praise to the LORD God of Israel.

LORD, when You went out from Seir,
When You marched from the field of Edom,
The earth trembled and the heavens poured,
The clouds also poured water;

The mountains gushed before the LORD,
This Sinai, before the LORD God of Israel.

In the days of Shamgar, son of Anath,
In the days of Jael,
The highways were deserted,
And the travelers walked along the byways.

Village life ceased, it ceased in Israel,
Until I, Deborah, arose,
Arose a mother in Israel.

They chose new gods;
Then there was war in the gates;
Not a shield or spear was seen among forty thousand in Israel.

My heart is with the rulers of Israel
Who offered themselves willingly with the people.
Bless the LORD!

Judges 5:1-9

Awake! Arise, Deborahs! As a fully functioning Body, may we gain the strategies of heaven, work together to bring those plans to earth, and see fear and terrorism defeated in our own day. Let us begin by humbling ourselves and listening to the Father's heart.

That Coming Day

Jesus is longing for a triumphant, strong, pure Bride — one who knows the Father's voice and enforces the victory He won at Calvary. It was a battle fought and a victory won through love, and it is through displaying His love (which includes His justice, mercy, kindness, goodness) that we will win and enforce the victory over terror in our day. The reality of a good Father who longs to adopt us as His sons and daughters when we come to Him through the Son — this is the hope we carry, because The Prince of Peace came to bring joy and hope to the nations of the earth. "… 'and I will shake all nations, and they shall come to the Desire of All Nations, and I will fill this temple with glory,' says the LORD of hosts." (Haggai 2:7).

In light of this prophetic picture, I can easily imagine Jesus, a beaming Bridegroom, proudly watching His Bride walk down the aisle. At that moment, all that The Church has become will bring pride and joy to his heart, and as we spend eternity praising Him for allowing us to participate in His glory here on earth, the pride and joy He feels for each of us will never dim or fade. The climax of this love story will surely be the day that we, as His Bride, lay our crowns at His feet in total adoration and worship. What a day that will be!

SIX

Securing Our Position

The reports of my death are greatly exaggerated.

Mark Twain

Over the past 15 years or so, my husband Jim and I have worked in restricted access nations in which Christians and missionaries are not welcome and have in the past been martyred. We've also worked on the border of a few closed nations, where the reigning attitude toward foreigners, Christians in particular, might be summed up as "Ready, shoot, aim." In other words, we've needed to know before we arrived who was friend, who was foe and how to tell the difference. As Deborah did, we needed the ability to "lean in and listen" to Papa God's heart in order to know how to proceed. There were a few occasions when we quickly removed ourselves from a situation that could have gone wrong because we knew that a certain person was not our friend. Other times, as we waited on God, He gave us a clear

An Unclouded Sun

understanding of what to do. The following story recounts one of those times.

Knowing the Time

Our schedule was made and we were happily envisioning a reunion with our friends in a distant village. Monday morning, bright and early, we would walk to the bus station and begin our travel to a village where a small group of believers had grown up from a single convert. We were looking forward to the privilege of sharing a day of Biblical training with the group.

Late Sunday afternoon the news was translated for us: the local police force had put a bounty on anyone evangelizing or spreading the gospel, and they were offering a full month's pay for anyone caught and turned in. The offer was serious and tempting enough to the locals that pastors had even warned their parishioners not to take the bait and turn anyone in.

Our spiritual son David told us of the warning with dispirited eyes. He, too, had been looking forward to the day of learning, because he was to serve as our translator in the village. We prayed together that God would show us what to do, and we went to sleep for the night.

When we awoke the next morning and had not heard a direct "no" from the Lord, we decided to proceed as planned, but with extra caution. Our conviction was that Jesus had told us to "go," which was what we would do until we heard "no."

Our senses were on full alert at the bus station as we stood in the long line of fellow passengers. We were praying under our breath, asking God to show us clearly how to proceed. Our concern was more for those we would visit than for ourselves. Suddenly David exclaimed, "Oh! I had a dream last night and I think it might be important!" With our encouragement, he shared his dream with us:

In the dream, he was with us when he looked to the ground and saw a watch. He picked it up to discover that it was the most beautiful watch ever made; no watch on earth could ever be so lovely. He turned it over and saw that on the back of it was inscribed the most wonderful love story ever told. He handed me the watch. Then he awoke.

Yes! This was our answer. In the form of a dream we felt the Lord was telling us it was time to go and tell the most beautiful love story ever: the story of Jesus. We purchased our tickets, and the sun seemed a bit brighter as we stepped out to board the bus.

If you had been watching with natural eyesight, you'd have said that nothing special happened that day. But we all knew better. We listened, we went, we loved and shared hearts as a family in God. On that fullness-of-time day, the Kingdom of God advanced throughout a village, and fear was replaced by hope as Papa's love was secured in each of our hearts.

Defining the Battle

Jim and I have always been very aware that people are not our problem or our enemy. Many years ago I set about memorizing the book of Ephesians, one of my favorite Bible books. While I can't quote it exactly word for word, I do have its precepts deeply hidden in my heart. One that stands out in relation to our discussion here is from chapter 6:

> *Put on the whole armor of God, that you may be able to stand against the wiles of the devil. For we do not wrestle against flesh and blood, but against principalities, against powers, against the rulers of the darkness of this age, against*

spiritual hosts of wickedness in the heavenly places.
                                                            Ephesians 6:11, 12

It's important that we always refer to our "enemy" as a specifically singular one. We, the church and Bride of Christ, have only one enemy, the same one that our Bridegroom made a spectacle of at the cross. Colossians 2:15 reads: "Having disarmed principalities and powers, He made a public spectacle of them, triumphing over them in it." Not only did Jesus disarm them (take away their weapons), but He then made sure that the news of His victory became public. "Spectacle" here relates to an object of contempt, or something exhibited publicly as unusual or notable. "Spectacle" can also refer to eyeglasses, or that which helps us see what our natural vision might miss. Jesus didn't want us to miss this: He defeated the devil. The devil — Satan, Lucifer or whichever of his names you choose — is our enemy. Not our neighbors, not our in-laws, not someone of a different nationality or religious belief from ours. This is an important truth, and one we often miss.

We also need to remember that Deborah didn't work alone. She determined exactly who the enemy was and then called the troops to action against him. And from the story we know that as each member of God's army (family) carried out his or her respective role in the drama, peace was secured for a nation. Being part of an army should remind us that we are not called to fight our battles or live in victory on our own. We need the strength and counsel of others. If we are to enforce the victory that Christ won through His death and resurrection, we must do it together.

In order to secure our positions, that is, to see our homes and our city streets become safe havens of refuge, it is vital that we know what the Lord is asking us to do and not do in any given situation. We must be very clear about who our enemy is and is not, and like

Deborah, we must work with others in the Body of Christ as we do God's will on earth.

A Clear Report

In May of 2011, thoughts of enemies and terrorism and Sisera converged in my mind while I was on my way to Pennsylvania to hold a Potter's Delight Women's Advance, which is based on Judges 4 and 5. Just before I flew there, the U.S. media was filled with the breaking news that Osama bin Laden, considered the number one terrorist leader and enemy of The United States, had been killed. Some rejoiced and some did not, but news stories made it clear that his compound in Afghanistan had been raided by America's Navy Seals Special Forces, and that his dead body had been buried at sea.

Whatever each individual thought, the general consensus seemed to be an overall sense of relief — a collective sigh, if you will — from the American people. Public enemy number one was dead. Surely terrorism against us was now weakened and the web of terror that bin Laden had spun was quickly beginning to erode. And yet, within hours came conflicting reports questioning the initial report and suggesting that he wasn't really dead. Someone had indeed been killed in his compound, but questions were posed again and again through news media. How could we be sure it was he? Was there indisputable proof? Could we relax? Were we sure? These questions soon faded away, and doubts about his death quieted. For a few days, though, our "rejoicing" at the death of our enemy was tempered by the fear that the report of his death was perhaps untrue.

One of the things I love about the Bible's story of Deborah is the description of Jael taking Sisera out. I don't like the gruesomeness of it, but rather that it leaves no room for doubt about the demise of the worst terrorist of his day: "At her [Jael's] feet he [Sisera] bowed, he fell, he lay down; at her feet he bowed, he fell: where he bowed, there he fell down dead" (KJV, Judges 4:27). Now, that's a pretty clear news report! No room is left for doubt or a conflicting report. In case you didn't get it the first time, you surely will believe it by the time you finish the verse!

Why does this matter? One reason is that we need to know not only who our enemy is, but that he's already been defeated. If the entire enemy army is wiped out, as was the case with Sisera's forces, we can rest assured that while the enemy himself walks about "as a roaring lion," the True Lion of the Tribe of Judah is the triumphant King. Knowing our enemy Satan was defeated and made a spectacle of at the cross, we can now walk in the victory Christ won there. Taking the Kingdom of Heaven into all the earth, we can expect to do greater things than He did, according to His promise in John 1:12: "Most assuredly I say to you, he who believes in Me, the works that I do he will do also; and greater works than there he will do, because I go to My Father."

We Have What It Takes

Jael, by virtue of the time and circumstances of her life as a nomadic woman, knew how to use a tent peg. When Sisera the terrorist was in her home, she did what came naturally and used what was "at hand," and when she did, she sent shock waves of victory that vibrated throughout the land. Her day-to-day skills led to a moment of destiny.

What about you? What is in your hand? A pen? A stethoscope? A dry-erase marker? A garden tool? A diaper? A measuring spoon? A paint brush? A book, a power tool, an iPad, a steering wheel? I hope

Securing Our Position

ing to get excited about who you are and what you
because both are "enough" when you allow the Lord
use you. Remember, we aren't talking about using our
abilities against people, but against the enemy of our

,tory of Sisera's death I hear echoes of Eden, where the
)hesied to the serpent, "And I will put enmity between
the woman, and between your offspring and hers; he will
ur head, and you will strike his heel" (NIV, Genesis 3:15).
se foretells the coming of Jesus, who would crush the head
n once and for all by suffering on the cross, dying and rising
ir ictory over death and the grave.

hat Jael's nailing of Israel's enemy to the ground within
prophetic picture of what would one day be finished
all by Jesus on the cross. It is also a picture of how
co-labor with Jesus in this Kingdom life. Just as Barak could
ve gone to battle without Deborah, Jesus had all He needed to
:feat the enemy without us. That He wants to work with us to
enforce His victory here on the earth should reinforce within us
an understanding of how secure we are in His love. When we feel
secure, we have hope.

Jael had everything she needed to do all that was required of her. So do you.

If you haven't yet realized what your gift or talent is, or if you're not sure that you can be used by God — sorry! No excuses for you, because aside from what you have in your hand, you have your own hand, which scripture describes as effective even if it's empty! In Judges 4:21, where we learn that Jael drove the tent peg into Sisera's temple, the word "drove" is the Hebrew word taqa (taw-kah'), which means to clatter, to slap the hands together; to drive a nail or tent peg, to fasten, pitch a tent, smite, strike. (New Strong's Exhaustive Concordance, #8628) Did you catch that? Clapping your hands is part of the definition given for what Jael did: she struck a tent peg into the enemy! Have you ever wondered why you should give in and clap during worship or intercession? Wow, this could change our way of thinking about hand-clapping in church! Along with singing the powerful words of worship, we can clap our hands and drive a nail through the devil's head – spiritually speaking, of course!

In the amazing ways of the God who is creator, even our empty hands can be lifted in worship to give Him praise and chase away our enemy. If you are experiencing any form of terror in your home or relationships, why not give it a try? It can't hurt, it may help, and if the neighbors hear, they'll just think you're watching a football game on television!

Peace and Rest

Barak, meanwhile, is still searching for Sisera, his one remaining foe and the general of the opposing army. After she had killed Sisera, Jael went out and called to Barak, basically saying that she had Sisera nailed down so he wouldn't get away.

So God kept His promise to Deborah that He would subdue Jabin, king of Canaan, and the children of Israel witnessed it. Did you catch that? When God kept His promise to Deborah, He demonstrated to the nation His heart's longing for a return to right relationship with His people. By keeping His promise and defeating the enemy, God made a way for the nation of Israel to live in peace with each other and with Him. He created a momentum in which the nation began turning back to Him, remembering Whose they were and joining Him in battle against the enemy. "And the hand of the children of Israel grew stronger and stronger against Jabin King of Canaan, until they had destroyed Jabin king of Canaan" (Judges 4:24).

After King Jabin was defeated, "the land [people] had rest for forty years" (Judges 5:31). Forty years equals a generation. An entire generation lived in rest without fear because three individuals trusted God and worked together to defeat terrorism and godlessness. Once again God's showed His good heart toward us when He called the land and His people, who are made from the earth, to a season of rest.

In each generation the Spirit of God calls for spiritual mothers and fathers to awake and arise in the land! He wants us to sing a song of victory when our enemy is defeated. He wants us — you — to hear His heart and to know His strategies for a victorious life. He wants your life to be all He intended it to be — for your family to be restored and healed and set free. He wants your land to enjoy rest and peace for the next generation.

Knowing the Father's heart — knowing that He is good and that He is for us — is the starting point for walking in both victory and rest. Then the question of who rules the land — our God or our enemy — has nothing to do with our abilities or lack of them. When God rules a land, He does it through us, and co-reigning with Him is based on knowing Whose we are and where we belong.

You see, most of us have been told and believed something like this our entire lives:

First, we need to Believe,

Then Change

In order to Belong.

But the heart of Father God is different. You already belong in His heart. As you believe in Jesus as Lord and Savior and live your life connected to Him, your journey is one of becoming all you were created to be.

On a Clear Day

I trust you find comfort and courage in knowing the Lord created you just the way He wants you to be. He isn't disappointed in the way you turned out! He doesn't wish you were cuter or that He'd made your nose smaller or your teeth whiter or your earlobes shorter. He's quite pleased with His creation. He sent Jesus to go through hell so you could have relationship with Him as His child, and He considers it all worth it.

God longs to help you remember and recover what was lost when sin clouded the sun in Eden. You are His, always and completely. No matter what your talents and abilities are, no matter what is or isn't in your hand, I invite you to believe that Jesus has unclouded the sun for you, personally. Scripture tells us "no creature is hidden from His sight, but all things are naked and open to the eyes of Him to whom we must give account" (Hebrews 4:13).

When you look around and all you can see are 900 chariots made of iron, how do you maintain hope? Help is available. We find it at His throne of mercy, and we are invited to enter into His presence boldly. "Let us therefore come boldly to the throne of grace, that we may obtain mercy and find grace to help in time of need" (Hebrews 4:16).

Using strength found in His presence, use your voice as Deborah did to speak and declare truth into your situation. Use your voice to sing your song, and expect the atmosphere around you to change. Deal with the fear and despair in your home by declaring truth from the word of God. Take what God has put in your hand, thank Him for it and ask Him for the strategy to use it for securing peace in your life. Expect your words to make a difference as you live life out loud. Be the "body part" that you were created to be, and lend your strength to the Body of Christ with whom you are connected. Knowing that faith, hope and love are the three things that remain, ask for an increase of faith, and practice learning how to love well. If you do, Hope will follow along.

Jesus taught us to pray: "Our Father in heaven, holy is your name. Your kingdom come, your will be done *on earth as it is in heaven*" (Matthew 6: 9-10; Italics mine). Don't settle for what is. Pull heaven to earth and secure peace and rest for the future. Your hope rests on the knowledge that it's what He wants.

It's time.

SEVEN

Tuning In To God's Voice

*Never be afraid to trust an unknown future
to a known God.*

Corrie TenBoom

My dad did love to talk. He loved words and could sit for hours, carrying on a conversation. No one was a stranger to him for long, as his gift of gab invited many into the influence of his life. But as much as he loved visiting with people on his front porch swing, Dad didn't like talking on the phone very much. Phone conversations are not my favorite thing, either, so when my parents were still alive, we called each other "now and then." We stayed in touch enough to be sure that everyone was doing well; we just weren't the kind that needed daily or even weekly phone conversations.

But when the phone rang and it was Dad, I always knew who it was as soon as I heard his voice. Even in the old days before caller ID, once I picked up the phone and heard, "Well, hello, there!" never did I need ask who was calling. No matter whether it had been days, weeks or longer (as when I traveled or lived overseas) since we talked, I always, always, always knew my father's voice. I'd been hearing it since before my birth; its tone and pitch and lilt were built into my very DNA, and my ears were tuned in to the timbre that was his alone. Sitting or standing beside him in church, I'd often fake saying the Apostle's Creed or just mouth the words to a hymn so I could hear his voice instead of my own. I felt deep comfort and safety when I heard Dad's voice ringing and singing out the praises of God. It was easy to feel secure with my dad by my side, declaring his love for God. I loved my daddy's voice.

Tune Your Dial to Hope

I also love God's voice. Whether you have been tuning in to what He is saying your entire life or you've just realized that He still speaks today, I encourage you to tune in and listen. His "station" plays music with rhythms of the hope that we long for.

We've already mentioned that God's word, The Bible, is alive and speaks to us. It's the "direct line" to His voice. Jesus made it very clear that it is natural for God's children to know His voice. The sound of it, the resonance of it – both are built into our spiritual DNA when we are born again.

> *He calls his own sheep by name and leads them out. And when he brings out his own sheep he goes before them, the sheep follow him, for they know his voice. Yet they will by no means follow a stranger, but will flee from him, for they do not know the voice of strangers.*
>
> John 10:3-5

Whether you're a long-time Christian, a new believer or a seeker, I want to encourage you: please, please, please read your Bible. Many available translations are easy to read, and they contain commentaries that help us put what God is saying into both historical and modern perspectives. Before starting to read, ask Holy Spirit to help you understand what God has to tell you through the printed Word, and suddenly it will come alive to you. You will "hear" in your heart and mind His great love, His great peace, His great, hopeful heart.

I try to read the Word of God every day, not as a religious ritual but as a love letter from my Dad, for in reality, that's exactly what it is: my heavenly Father's heart and love put into print for me to read, read and read again. When something difficult is going on in my life or I need clear direction, I read until He speaks. Sometimes that involves a few minutes of reading, while other times it requires most of a day —or perhaps most of a year - reading, processing as I go about my day, going back and reading again, but not giving up or giving in until I hear my Father's voice. For me, personally, the Psalms, Isaiah and Ephesians are the books where I often hear His voice. I underline verses that speak to me and write the date beside them; they are a testimony of His faithfulness to me, and when I go through another challenge, I am often encouraged by my written reminder of what Papa has already told me through His Word. Our Heavenly Father loves to speak to us every day through the Bible, and knowing no strangers, He invites us all into His embrace.

Don't worry. He has your number and can get in touch anytime He wants. It's mostly a matter of our taking time to listen, which is a key to keeping hope alive.

Say What?

God calls (speaks to) us a lot. I know this because I've heard Him call me a lot, and He's not a respecter of persons. His voice doesn't always come through the Bible; it is often Spirit-to-spirit communication. Sometimes He pricks our consciences, or He'll make sure that we have a niggling sense that something just isn't right. Oftentimes He speaks through the voice of a friend or family member. While we are not to live in a spirit of fear, a natural fear of real danger is one that way God's Spirit warns us and keeps us safe.

Whether out of rebellion, extreme tiredness, or a myriad of other reasons, there are times when I really don't want to listen. When we choose to ignore, deny or turn our back on His call, hearing loss begins. Thankfully, He is a master at reversing hearing loss in both the natural and spiritual! Repenting, changing our mind about ignoring His voice, confessing that we have been wrong to ignore His call and then turning our ear toward His voice again are all steps to reversing spiritual hearing loss. Holy Spirit is quick to come with the comfort of His forgiveness, and He is the best Hearing Aide in the world!

Peripheral Hearing

There are times when God speaks something to me, and I know it's just for me, rather like the phone game that my earthly dad and I used to play when I was a little girl. Even if I'd just come from being with him, when Daddy and I were ready to hang up he'd say, "I love you!" and I'd reply, "I love you more!" He'd respond, "No way! I love you most!" which I would then refute through giggles and insist that, indeed, I loved him more than he loved me. (It remains a delightfully unresolved issue to this day.) That conversation was just between my dad and me, and no one knew about it except us.

There are other times when God speaks to the body of Christ as a whole. I believe one such time occurred earlier this spring when both my husband and I suddenly had severe earaches. I knew something interesting was going on, first of all because we had no symptoms of allergies or colds, and also because we aren't prone to earaches and don't usually suffer from them. So while we treated the symptoms, I asked the Lord to tell me if He was trying to teach us a greater lesson.

Within days we learned that many friends, scattered all over the country, were experiencing the same symptoms. The medical community offered no cure; rather, doctors suggested simply treating the symptoms. While I'm not prepared to turn this into theology, I thought I heard Him say that He was fine-tuning our eardrums so that we could hear His voice more clearly.

Many voices have been prophesying "new sounds" coming from heaven, specifically sounds of worship. I don't doubt that new sounds are coming, and I plan to hear them. I also think that we have failed to hear many "old sounds" and plenty of the nuances of God's voice, because our ears have not been attuned hear them. Just as a drummer occasionally needs to check the drum head and stretch it to correct the pitch, so the Lord may have been recalibrating our eardrums to His voice. I'm not saying that God gave us all earaches! What I am saying is that perhaps He used whatever was going around to speak a truth to us — if we were listening.

I've also been captivated by the idea of peripheral hearing. I know that there is no such a thing. I made up the term, but it seems to me that just as we can catch a glimpse of something out of the corner of our eye, we might be able to catch a sound of His Spirit's movement out of the "corner of our ear." I'm not sure if it's real or not, but it's my theory, so I keep my ears on alert to prevent missing something when it's just out of my natural hearing's range. I want to hear everything He has to say to me.

I invite you to try peripheral hearing with me, and lets just see if we can hear His voice more clearly, coming from an angle we've not experienced it, previously. I know that God restores hearing loss. With all the unknowns of the future, we can rest securely in the knowledge that we hear our Father's voice. Knowing that He wants us to hear the sounds of heaven and then express them on earth gives me great hope for good in the days to come.

God's Unconventional Ways

Before you decide that my hearing loss theory is just too far out, consider with me that God's ways are "other" than ours, and very often unconventional. Why do we read the Bible stories about all kinds of wild and new ways God did things (such as speaking through a donkey, causing an ax head to float, or having a virgin give birth to Jesus), but think that in our day His ways should come in neat packages, shrink-wrapped for safety, instructions included? He's just not that small. He doesn't fit in our box.

Chapters 6 and 7 of 2 Kings contain an example of God's unique way of doing things. This story about four lepers takes place in the days of the prophet Elisha. Surrounded by the king of Syria's armed forces, Samaria was in the midst of a severe famine, and the little bit of available food came at a hugely inflated price. In fact, the people were so desperate that some had turned to cannibalism.

When the king of Samaria heard of this travesty, he became enraged at the prophet Elisha and wanted him dead. The Lord spoke to Elisha and warned him of the plot to kill him. When the king's messenger came to Elisha's door, the prophet declared what He was hearing the Lord tell him: within 24 hours the famine would be ended and food prices back to normal. One of the king's men scoffed at this and declared that even if heaven's windows opened and rained down food, this wouldn't be possible. Because he doubted the word of the Lord and spoke against it, Elisha told him that he would see it with his eyes but would not be able to eat any of the food that was coming.

The scene then changes to four men who sat at the city's entrance gate. These men were lepers and therefore were not permitted to enter. Starving and desperate, they devised a plan. Instead of waiting around to die of starvation, they decided to take their chances with the Syrian army, which was wealthy and well supplied with food and drink. Even if the Syrian soldiers were to kill them, at least their deaths would be swift.

At twilight they started off on foot toward the camp of the Syrian forces. Imagine their shock and wonder when they arrived at the outer edges of the Syrian camp to discover that no one was there! Not even a sentry to guard the camp or a runner to relay a message to the commander.

The four lepers went into the camp and ate and drank their fill! In one tent after another they found food and drink for the taking. And just as incredibly, they helped themselves to clothing, silver and gold. Suddenly, one leper's conscience kicked in, and he realized that they were keeping a day of celebration to themselves. Not willing to face the punishment that would surely be theirs if they remained silent about the bounty, they returned to let the king know what they had found. Because they weren't permitted to enter the city, they called out the good news to the gatekeepers, who of course passed it on to the king.

The king, awakened by this news in the night, was skeptical and thought it was a ruse by the Syrians to trap the starving Samaritans when they ran out to get the food. He sent a scouting party, who returned with confirmation that the lepers had told the truth, and that even the road was littered with the clothing and weapons that the Syrian army had thrown away during their hasty retreat.

It's hard to imagine how quickly and passionately word spread throughout the town! Food! Starving people suddenly found a burst of strength and ran to the Syrian outpost. Because of the sudden abundance of food, prices instantly dropped to pre-famine rates. And the man who had scoffed at the word of the Lord? He was the man that the king had appointed to be in charge of the gate. The crazed-with-hunger mob trampled him on their way to get food, so the word came true that he would hear of the miracle but not partake of it.

An Army of Four

An amazing story, isn't it? But I purposely skipped over one of the best parts so I could highlight it here. You see, the reason that the Syrian army fled as fast as they could is that when the four lepers limped toward the Syrian camp,

> ... the Lord had caused the army of the Syrians to hear the noise of chariots and the noise of horses — the noise of a great army; so they said to one another, "Look, the king of Israel has hired against us the kings of the Hittites and the kings of the Egyptians to attack us!
>
> 2 Kings 7:6-7

Therefore they arose and fled at twilight, and left their camp behind — intact, complete with tents, horses, and donkeys — and they fled for their lives.

Are you kidding me?! Leprosy is a debilitating disease, as we all know. People who have it lose limbs and therefore their mobility. And yet four men — not four Samsons or four Davids, but four lepers — sounded like two armies to the enemy of Israel. How is that possible? Verse 7 tells us that the Lord caused them to sound that way in the Syrian's ears.

I don't know how big the armies of the Hittites or the army of the Egyptians were, but I think it's safe to guess that we're talking a large number of armed forces, here. I've also never heard the sound of an army's worth of chariots and horses, but surely that much horse power and that many chariots would make the very ground rumble when on the attack. And that's what four lepers sounded like to one of the largest armies on earth at the time.

I call that an unconventional intervention of God. A God who cannot be contained in a box of my making gives me hope for my future.

Supernatural Math

Although set during a time of divine judgment against the backslidden nation of Israel, Deuteronomy 32:30 gives us a principle of spiritual warfare worth looking at. It states that, with the Lord's intervention, one person can put a thousand enemies to flight and two people can put ten thousand to flight. Neither old nor new math took this into consideration when I was in school. Unfortunately, neither did the church. Earlier in the passage, the Lord clearly states that He doesn't want anyone to misunderstand who has been at work in this situation; He wants no one but Himself to get the credit when He says, "lest their adversaries should misunderstand, lest they should say, 'our hand is high, and it is not the Lord who has done all this' " (Deuteronomy 32:27). God points out the impossible odds of two people defeating ten times more enemies than one for the purpose of showing that only He can cause things that don't add up to happen.

Once again I see hints of God's presence and glory in the battle that Deborah and Barak waged against Jabin's forces. Using God's supernatural math, Deborah alone could have routed one thousand soldiers, but we know that Jabin had 10,000 troops. When the woman Deborah and the man Barak acted on God's word and worked together for His purposes, the two of them put all ten thousand to flight, and when the Gentile woman Jael did her part, the final blow was dealt to the enemy.

The Word makes it clear that God works such miracles when His people turn toward Him and live according to His ways, which can only happen when God's heart becomes man's home. Psalm 91: 7 tells us that "A thousand may fall at your side, and ten thousand at your right hand, but it shall not come near you." Why? Verse 9 tells us: "Because you have made the Lord, who is my refuge, even the Most High, your dwelling place."

We read in the book of Acts that when the church was a newborn entity, the disciples of Jesus were all in one place and in one accord. If four lepers under the Old Covenant sounded like two armies advancing for battle when they walked together for a common purpose, what do you suppose the enemy hears when we, on the New Covenant side of the cross, set our hearts to walk in one accord? If we could only grasp the authority we have as sons and daughters of God Most High! When that understanding comes, and it is coming, we surely will do greater things than Jesus did, just as He foretold.

I think I'm finally starting to like math.

Be Careful, Little Ears

Discernment is vital when we listen to God's voice. To be regarded as truth, what we hear must line up with the Bible, because the Word of God is the standard. This underscores the importance of knowing the Bible. We must know what it says from our own reading — not just from accepting what others tell us it says. Scripture is the plumb line against which we measure what we hear.

Not all the thoughts that we think in a day are our own. Become aware of what you're thinking. Thoughts that are contrary to the word of God are to become captives of God's word. (2Corinthians 10:5) When the enemy comes knocking at the tent flap of your mind, don't invite him in and serve him tea! Kris Vallotton, a prophetic voice at Bethel Church in Redding, California, says that the enemy only knows our thoughts when we think the thoughts that he gives us. If we entertain the enemy's thoughts long enough, they become ours. When tempted by Satan in the wilderness, Jesus didn't consider whether or not the enemy's words had any validity. Instead, He instantly used the Word of God to shut down Satan's lies. With Jesus as our example, we also use the sword of the Spirit, which is the word of God, to send the enemy packing. Jael killed Sisera by delivering a head wound; we destroy enemy-inspired thoughts by "nailing them to the cross," that is, by handing them over to Jesus and accepting His thoughts in exchange.

The way we respond when God speaks to us is extremely important. When He tells us something that seems impossible, we must respond with faith. Zechariah, the father of John the Baptist, and Mary, the mother of Jesus, were both told that they would have sons, and though one was natural and one was virginal, each conception was possible only through a miracle of God. Both Zechariah and Mary knew that conception was naturally impossible, and both asked how such a thing could happen. Zechariah asked through the lens of doubt, and he was struck speechless until the baby was born. Mary asked through the lens of awestruck wonder and then sang a song of praise. We can see that it's okay to ask questions when God speaks, but it's important to ask them in faith. Asking with doubt clouds our understanding of His power to do the impossible.

Without miracles we have an incomplete revelation of our Father God, so it's important that we hear Him accurately and well, then respond in faith that He can perform the impossible. Abraham had faith for his miracle and it was counted to him as righteousness. Jesus did the works of His father: he performed miracles, saying that He only did what He saw the Father doing and only spoke what He heard the Father saying. He lived on earth and in the Kingdom at the same time, and His miracles displayed the Father's heart for us.

God's intervention in our lives, through the miracle of salvation or physical healing, the wonder of hearing His voice, or any other way He chooses to break into our lives, is for our benefit and our good. His Word and His ways give us abundant reason to hold onto hope!

Love's Response

When we sing songs of love and praise to God, we are joining our voices with those of Deborah and Barak, Moses and Miriam, Zechariah and Mary and multitudes more. As our praises ascend, God is so attracted to the sound that He comes and rests there.

No one except my very young children has ever asked me to sing. It's a miracle for me to think that the God of the universe, the I Am, All Sufficient One, wants to hear my song.

Equally striking is that He sings over me. He sings! Over me! Not despite me or when He's coincidentally in my vicinity. He deliberately sings over me — happy songs of rejoicing from my Father's voice, sung as He holds me in His embrace. "The Lord your God is in your midst, The Mighty One will save. He will rejoice over you with gladness. He will quiet you with His love. He will rejoice over you with singing" (Zephaniah 3:17). He sings to make me glad, to quiet my soul, to invite me to rejoice along with Him. To hope again.

I think I'll just be quiet for a moment and listen as He sings. Hope is rising as I listen and feel secure in the shadow of His presence.

I love my Father's voice.

EIGHT

We Need A Bigger Tent

God stretches out the heavens like a canopy, and spreads them out like a tent to live in.

The Prophet Isaiah

If anyone finds the tiger balm, the box holding Jim's jean shorts or the rest of our DVD's, please let us know. It seems that every time we move, things get lost, and these are all on the missing items list from our last move – the third move in two years. We were glad that we knew where both vehicles were when the dust settled.

The reasons people move are as numerous and varied as the people themselves. For me, certain parts of the moving process are exciting. It's like starting off on a new adventure, whether across town, across the country or across the globe. I like adventure, but having made each of these kinds of moves, I've had enough adventure for awhile, and I'm ready to settle in right where we are. During the course of the last move, I wrote the following in my journal, to express what was in my heart:

> *I am beginning to understand moving. I feel a bit like a nomad, pulling up stakes and heading out again. There's an excitement in the change, new views, new vistas, new friends and neighbors. The opportunity to transform an empty house into a full, warm, welcoming home. A chance to settle down for awhile in a permanent home, to stay in one place.*

For people in less modern times, moving was different. I put my belongings in boxes and then into a truck, but Jael rolled her home up and carried it with her on camel back. Pilgrims left all their worldly possessions behind and boarded a ship with others like themselves, all with their own baggage of fear and uncertainty. Oh, the courage those women possessed! How many landed in America only to end up destitute or worse? I see them as giving up their lives so their children and grandchildren would have it better than they did.

I stand in awe of the pioneer women, whose temporary homes were covered wagons— covers of canvas to withstand the heat and humidity of the Midwest, the driving, endless winds of Kansas, the scorching desert sun of the west. No interstate highway system, no air conditioned hotels along the way. Of such stock heroes are made.

In the course of our recent moves, I have sometimes found myself, as my predecessors did, experiencing a temporary uncertainty about where home was. I felt pressured by an innate need to be safe and to nest, and I saw no welcoming tree branch anywhere. I yearned to belong not only to someone but to a place. My taproot of security seemed exposed and vulnerable — searching, longing, waiting for fertile soil in which to plant itself. I wanted to go home but wasn't sure where home was.

For each wanderer, for each sojourner longing for home, Hope becomes the North Star. It is toward hope and in hope that we all journey. Hope is our reason for leaving all that we have known, hope is our traveling companion, and hope is our destiny and guide.

Today I remember hope. I look hope in the face and find courage to go on. I follow hope, I cling to hope, I rejoice in hope and on hope I lean.

Hope remains. Hope does not disappoint.

Company's Coming

Isaiah 54:1 reminds me of the promise God gave to Sarah when she was yet barren:

> *"Sing, O barren, you who have not borne! Break forth into singing, and cry aloud, you who have not labored with child! For more are the children of the desolate than the children of the married woman," says the Lord.*

I don't know all that is hidden for us in this verse, but I do know that the Lord is telling us to get ready for the arrival of children for whom we didn't labor. Prophetic voices have declared that we are living in the time of a billion-soul harvest. A billion. I can't comprehend how many that is, but I'm pretty sure I don't have enough dishes to serve them all. What I mean is that the Kingdom is about to advance at a rate we've never seen before, and we, the church, will need resources of every kind with which to feed, nourish and grow these new believers.

If God is bringing lots of children, it makes sense that we'll need a bigger house. Directly following this promise of many offspring, verses 2-3 of Isaiah 54 reads:

> *Enlarge the place of your tent, and let them stretch out the curtains of your dwelling: Do not spare.*
>
> *Lengthen your cords, and strengthen your stakes.*
>
> *For you shall expand to the right and to the left, and your descendants will inherit the nations, and make the desolate cities inhabited.*

The Lord gave His people the blessing of knowing that many people were coming, and then He reminded them that a bigger tent would be necessary to accommodate the blessing. I believe that He's telling us the same thing today.

My point is not to dissect the passage, but rather to look at the implications of kingdom expansion. Today, if we need more room in our homes, we either move to a larger house or add a room. In Old Testament days, it seems that a room addition was the order of the day. From the previous verses we can see that expansion required more curtains to use as walls, longer cords for tethering the tent, and stronger stakes. With the added weight and tension of more curtains and longer stretches of cord, the tent pegs would need to be more substantial before they were pounded into solid ground.

John 1:14 tells us that Jesus came to tabernacle (dwell) among us. We don't use the word "tabernacle" in this way today, but it signified His coming to make His home with us — to camp out. As the Old Testament tabernacle was a place of protection and communion for the Israelites, so Jesus is for us. At the same time, we are called the temple of God in 1 Corinthians 3:16: "Do you not know that you are the temple of God and that the Spirit of God dwells in you?"

When Jesus was ready to go home to heaven, He commissioned us to go into all the world and preach the Gospel to every creature (Matthew 28). The tent, the place of His dwelling or habitation, was to be taken into all the world as His people extended the Kingdom. The tabernacle of Moses was put up and taken down as the children of Israel went through the wilderness, so that the Presence of God, the place of His dwelling, was always with them. Today, we who are the carriers of His Presence and the very temple of God, are to expand across the globe, taking His Spirit, resident within us, to the whole world. We aren't required to dismantle a physical tent and move it about; rather, where we go, He is.

This commission, far from being accomplished, is in fact still in process. As we go, and as the lost come home, we will need room to receive them. Not only will we need physical room in which to teach, train and disciple new believers in His ways, but our hearts and minds will also be required to adjust and make room for them. Any remaining veils of prejudice or apathy in our hearts must be removed and replaced with the weavings of His protection and care. As we are stretched in our ability to find the time and energy required to care for those being saved, it is imperative that we be anchored on the Rock of Jesus, and that our "tents" be secured by deep roots in His Word.

Beach-Size Promise

In our own strength we cannot work up enough compassion or love for anyone, let alone a billion souls. I believe the answer — the hope for us in this upcoming situation — can be found in a snippet about Solomon's life. In fact, the details are hidden and are easily passed over, but I believe they are gems of hope hidden for such a time as this.

The background is laid out in Genesis 22, which is the story of God testing Abraham by asking him to sacrifice Isaac. Isaac, the promised child for whom Abe and Sarah had waited so long, was now to be put to death on the altar at God's directive. Of course we know the Lord Himself provided a ram so that Isaac was not harmed, but nonetheless, Abraham sure did win this race of faith when he was put to the test. Verses 15-17 read:

Then the Angel of the Lord called to Abraham a second time out of heaven an said, "By Myself I have sworn, says the Lord, because you have done this thing, and have not withheld your son, your only son – blessing I will bless you, and multiplying I will multiply your descendants as the stars of the heaven and as the sand which is on the seashore; and your descendants shall possess the gate of their enemies."

In The Message verse 18 reads: "I'll bless you — oh, how I'll bless you! And make sure that your children flourish — like stars in the sky! Like sand on the beaches!"

Here again we see God's miracle math: With a heart of faith and hope, we offer Him that which matters most to us and He gives back to us more than we can count. God's heart is so inclined toward us, His love and goodness so abundant!

Skipping ahead, we find Jacob praying and reminding God of His promise in Genesis 32:12: "For You said, 'I will surely treat you well, and make your descendants as the sand of the sea, which cannot be numbered for multitude.' " Isaac was there when his father, Abraham, got the word from heaven that his descendants would be as numerous as sand. He obviously passed this story on to his son, Jacob, and here Jacob, who would be renamed "Israel" by God, is reminding God of the promise yet to be fulfilled.

Beach-Size Fulfillment

How do we know whether or not God fulfilled the promise made to Abraham and reiterated by Jacob/Israel? In 1 Kings 4 we learn some things about King Solomon, who reigned generations after Abraham, Isaac and Jacob. Verse 1 says that Solomon was king over all Israel, and we read in verse 20 that "Judah and Israel were as numerous as the sand by the sea in multitude, eating and drinking and rejoicing." He did it! The promise was fulfilled. What generations had hoped for was now a reality.

The chapter then goes on to explain how much food was needed for one day, for both man and beast. Makes my grocery bill look pretty insignificant. How in the world could any man know how to care for this many people? The key is found in verse 29: "And God gave Solomon wisdom and exceeding great understanding and *largeness of heart like the sand on the seashore*." (italics mine)

We see here that when Solomon asked God for wisdom to rule this vast number of people, God gave him even more. Not only did He give wisdom, but also "exceeding great understanding and largeness of heart like the sand on the seashore." In the tabernacle of Solomon's heart, God stretched out the curtains, lengthened the cords and strengthened the pegs so that he could attend to the welfare of each and every person in his kingdom. God expanded Solomon's heart with wisdom and understanding so that it fit the call he'd been given. He will surely do the same for you and me as we prepare for the greatest harvest of souls that the world has ever seen.

I believe that the command in Isaiah to "spare not" when enlarging our tent is our clue to understanding how inclusive this move of God is. As we ask for wisdom from heaven, we, too, will be given the blueprint for building the Kingdom in such a way that we will share the Gospel at any cost and give abundantly to see the lost and the orphaned come home to Papa's great love. Lord, expand our hearts, and give us wisdom and understanding to know how to prepare and build, ready and able to provide all that is needed. Help us to "spare not," and to think and plan in larger terms than we ever have before.

Where do we find the hope that God will answer our prayer for this? In Psalm 139:17-18: "How precious also are Your thoughts to me, O God! How great is the sum of them! If I should count them, they would be more in number than the sand. When I am awake, I am still with You." God thinks as many thoughts about you as there are grains of sand. His heart doesn't lack the capacity or compassion to give us all that is needed, and then some.

We, God's Spirit-carrying people, are His moveable church, and as His family of believers grows, we must enlarge our tents and our hearts. The bigger the church grows and the more the Kingdom of God expands, the more deeply grounded in truth and grace we must become. The God of Israel is the God of the whole earth. May His kingdom come and His will be done through us —His tents on earth — as it is in heaven.

Seeing in the Dark

Psalm 139:11-12, from The Message Bible: "Then I said to myself, 'Oh, He even sees me in the dark! At night I'm immersed in the light! It's a fact: darkness isn't dark to You; night and day, darkness and light, they're all the same to You.' "

Imagine: God can see in the dark without night-vision goggles! No matter how dark your circumstances seem right now or how dark the world around us becomes, God will never lose sight of us. He won't have to search for us in the darkness because He is light, and in Him there is no darkness at all. When He shows up, the very darkest situations on the planet are suddenly in plain view, exposed by an unclouded sun. We, His children, are the light of the world because His light is within us, and the same holds true for us: as we go into the world and carry His hope into hopeless situations, we can expect darkness to flee from the light of His wisdom and understanding. As people begin to awaken from the dark night of living apart from their Father, He promises to be the One who will lift their heads when they throw off their slumber and slavery to sin.

As our eyes adjust to the dawn of a new, hopeful day of Kingdom Presence, we will choose where to focus them. Whether we look at the natural circumstances around us or the supernatural reality available to us will determine how we think and speak. Knowing what He has named us, remembering Whose we are, we will have in our hands all that we need to lighten the load and mend the broken hearts of the hopeless.

While You Were Sleeping

Down through the ages, God has kept watch over us, whether we were asleep or awake and whether or not we were aware of His love. He has never nodded off, never taken a nap or forgotten where any of us were. His love for us never lessened while He watched over His sleepy bride and gently shook her awake.

His supernatural ways become natural to us when we walk in sonship. As we begin to believe the truth of the new names He has given us, we will also begin to walk in that identity. As our walk becomes a run, we will see the world and Kingdom from a clearer perspective. As we see Him more clearly, we will respond to His call to become more and allow Him to fulfill our inner longing to be all He created us to be.

God's heart for us is that we stretch ourselves to make room for Kingdom expansion. The book of Ephesians, chapter 4, tell us that apostles, prophets, evangelists, pastors and teachers were given to equip the believers — the saints — for the work of ministry and to build up the body of Christ, which is the church. These gifts are in operation, verse 13 says, "until we all come to the unity of the faith and of the knowledge of the Son of God, to a perfect man, to the measure of the stature of the fullness of Christ." (Italics mine.) God's intent is that we have the degree (measure) of maturity (stature) that will complete our knowledge of Who this Jesus is that we love and serve; He wants us to know this Father to whom we belong and this Spirit of God that dwells within us. Then we will no longer be tossed about as children, falling for the deceits of man, but will grow up into Christ, our Head. As we grow up and go out, His promise is that signs and wonders will follow. Kingdom expansion brings the miraculous and awakens us to God's heart for us.

Remembering God's faithfulness to His people through all the ages, we don't need to fear that we won't 'have what it takes' to bring in this harvest. The same Father God who expanded Solomon's heart is able to expand ours to fit the task at hand, as well. He has set the stage for us to walk into the harvest fields with joyous shouts of hope.

Open Arms for Gathering

Working in the villages of Asia for many years, I became accustomed to seeing crops harvested in ways that are now considered old-fashioned. I've watched dozens of farm workers descend on a field of ripe grain with sharpened scythes, and like a well-oiled machine, efficiently cut the grain, gather it into their arms and stack it into compact, picturesque bundles to be collected at a later time. First, all the grain was gathered and formed into a shock or bundle; later, the bundles were gathered and carried into a barn. The process of gathering the bundles always reminded me of a hug, because it looked as though the farmers were embracing the grain as they gathered it in.

I also lived in Iowa for many years, and although the local Amish families used a bit more equipment, their ways of harvesting were not much more sophisticated than the ones I witnessed in Asia. The Amish work hard to maintain their lifestyle, but they always seem to have plenty of strength and energy for the next task, so I started watching them work to see if I could find some gems to glean for myself. I learned that even though the Amish work long and hard hours, they eat a lot and eat well to sustain their energy and strength. The lack of electricity in their homes means that they aren't distracted by the internet or cable TV, and perhaps as important as anything else, they keep the Sabbath. Although this might be an "old, hard yoke" to many of us (and I'm not recommending the legalistic ways often associated with the Amish lifestyle), the point is that they enter into rest one day a week. All work stops, and for an entire day they focus on family, food, and most of all, worship.

For me, this is a good word picture for gathering the harvest of souls. As we learn to work from a place of rest, to eat well, to care for our physical bodies and to focus on God's unclouded face, He will give us willing arms to embrace the harvest, and He will enable our hearts to love those whom He gathers better than ever before. More than one billion souls are waiting to hear God's call and be adopted into the family of God. May we be those who scatter the seeds of the Gospel to all nations, then open our arms to welcome the orphans home.

We're going to need a bigger tent.

NINE

Walking In Hope

Oh, you're sure to do that [get somewhere] if you only walk long enough.

The Cheshire Cat,
Walt Disney's *Alice in Wonderland*

These shoes are made for walking, not for running. I made sure of that when I bought them. A delightful young man who appeared to have been on the planet a mere couple of decades actually asked me if I was buying shoes for walking or running. Really? Look at me and then ask me that again!

Running is highly overrated, in my humble opinion — at least the Colorado/California kind of running, where it's all about how long and how fast one runs and how suave one looks when doing it. Where I grew up, people only ran if they were being chased. Just a couple of years ago, when I moved from the Midwest, it was still that way. If I had told anyone in Iowa that I had started running, my statement would have been met with a gasp, a concerned look and the inevitable "Oh no! What happened? Who is after you? Can I do anything to help?" I remember seeing joggers prancing alongside the roadway and my father-in-law quipping, "Poor kid. Bet he wishes he had a car." Running just wasn't in vogue there.

Then I moved to California. Northern California. Once here, I was told by my nutritionist, that instead of just walking as I had been doing for years, I needed to add running. I'll spare you the ugly details of just how that looks; suffice it to say that the rumors of fog on the running trail are wrong. It's the icy jet contrail I leave behind when I pass by in my walking shoes.

And that's where the rub comes in. The response here in California when I've mentioned to friends that I've taken up running as a form of punishment, er, I mean exercise, has been a smug, all-knowing look that is always—and I mean always—followed by, "Ha! Are you running, or are you shuffling your feet and calling it running?"

Thankfully, I have had plenty of practice in the art of forgiveness, and these remarks afford me the opportunity to offer it once again. While I know that no harm is meant, what I could really use at this point is a bit of encouragement. You see, even though others might see my efforts as shuffling along, I view picking up my feet and putting them back down as steps of victory. I'm aware of what it costs to get up early and be on the trail (my first cup of strong coffee, for starters!), and I know the amount of determination I've needed to keep it up, day after day. Where others see a middle-aged woman puffing along the trail, in my mind's eye I envision an Olympic gold medal, flowers, cheering crowds — the entire package — each time I complete mile two. I'm not running a race to set a new time record, nor am I competing against anyone else's style or speed. This is my race, and I'm running it as best I can. Each step forward echoes "yes!" in my ears, and each gasp for breath tells me I'm awake and alive and pressing forward, not lagging behind. Muscles that ache cause tears not of pain, but of thanks that I have a body that still works and can still run — even in shoes that were made for walking.

I Believe I Can Fly

A number of western bluebirds make their homes in the trees along the trail where I run. They dart and dash back and forth around and in front of me, and I've come to think of them as my own little cheerleaders, dressed in blue. Birds, if you notice, don't mess around with walking or running when they want to get somewhere; they just take off and fly. As far back as our collective memory reaches, humanity has longed to fly like the birds. While I'm grateful for airplanes, it's obvious that we're a long way from true, free flight. (I've never heard of birds being delayed or on standby.) Even so, the lyrics of a 1970's song often come to mind when I am running: "I believe I can fly".

As much as we'd all love to take to the air, flying is just not how Creator God designed human beings. His plan for us is a walk of faith, not a flight of faith — step by step, sometimes walking, sometimes shuffling, sometimes running on the path we've chosen. I believe He is more interested in the fact that we are hungry for more of His Presence, thirsty to drink more deeply of the knowledge of Him, longing to know His heart and see His face, than He is in how we get there. If crawling into His Presence, exhausted and worn, is how we come, He delights in our coming. It's more about heading in His direction than about how fast we move or how suave we look while crawling. The invitation is simply, "Come."

Walking, — or Running — in Hope

What does walking or running have to do with hope? A lot, I believe.

The Bible refers to our attempts at loving the Lord our God — at hearing His voice and at following His ways — as our "walk" with God. Examples abound:

> *Therefore we were buried with Him through baptism into death, that just as Christ was raised from the dead by the glory of the Father, even so we also should walk in newness of life.*
>
> Romans 6:4, Italics mine

> *For we walk by faith, not by sight.*
>
> 2 Corinthians 5:7, Italics mine

> *And walk in love, as Christ also has loved us and given Himself for us, an offering and a sacrifice to God for a sweet-smelling aroma*
>
> Ephesians 5:2, Italics mine

> *He who says he abides in Him ought himself also to walk just as He walked.*
>
> 1 John 2:6, Italics mine

Our walk with God is also compared to a long-distance race by the apostle Paul in Hebrews 12:1: "… let us run with endurance the race that is set before us." When I feel unable to keep up with the race, my self-security is threatened, which allows fear, anxiety and hopelessness to slow me down. If I want to run the race with endurance, I must run with hope.

The ninth chapter of 1 Corinthians also refers to our Christian life as a race. Verse 24 says, "Do you not know that in a race all the runners run, but only one gets the prize? Run in such a way as to get the prize."

One of the ways we run successfully is to keep the finish line in sight—to keep our eyes on Jesus and not on our fellow runners. How easy it is to get caught up in who has the newest running shoes, the sweetest running gear or the most natural, smooth stride. I know from my limited running experience that I don't dare watch others who are running and compare myself to them. If I do, my goal becomes to be like them, and I'll surely quit on the spot when I can't compete with people who have been running for years or who were born running like gazelles.

Another person's successful race will usually inspire us to run longer and farther than we thought we could, and another's accomplishments gives us a standard to shoot for. When Rodger Bannister ran and broke the four-minute mile barrier, he opened the door for many who followed — not only to meet but to break his record. Running faster than any man had been recorded running before, he set a new standard, a new goal. What was considered impossible one moment before was now within reach of all runners.

If our goal is to finish our race well, another's testimony of greatness is often what we need to inspire us toward pressing on and accomplishing greater things for ourselves. However, if we lose our focus and hold up another's gift or ability as the only acceptable standard for making it to our own finish line, hope will vanish, and we're likely to quit trying and throw in the towel.

Each day that I get up and run, I win just because I did it. I can only compare myself with myself. Was I able to run a bit further today than I did yesterday? Am I less winded this week than last? When I compare myself with myself and gauge my progress that way, I have great hope that tomorrow and next week I'll be stronger and faster than I am today. Hope for improvement, hope for achieving goals in my life, hope that I'll cross the finish line I'm headed for on any given day — hope for all grows and blossoms and keeps me going.

Apostles and Prophets and Evangelists – Oh My!

In the past couple of decades, the church of Jesus Christ has once again experienced a revolution: the reestablishment of an apostolic and prophetic foundation. (Ephesians 4:11)

During the process, the names, faces and voices of many church leaders have become so well known that great numbers of people have learned and gleaned blessings from their God-given gifts. These men and women in leadership have been running the race they were given to run, heading toward the finish line by seeking God's presence and His face. In so doing, they attracted the attention of the "crowd." I'm so grateful for the sacrifices they have made, because they have encouraged, taught and challenged the church to love God more! In other words, they have broken through limitations that once seemed impenetrable, and in doing so have made finishing the race well seem a bit more within reach for all of us. In short, they've given us hope.

Unfortunately, we in the church have sometimes looked at the more stellar of our fellow runners, and rather than using their successes as inspiration to run our races, we have decided that we can never be as fast or as good. We feel that we'll never be able to run with the seemingly effortless stride we see in them, and we're well aware that we don't have the newest shoes or latest iPod to keep us running. Anybody relate to what I'm saying? It's so easy to look at those on the stage and decide that our own personal races are pretty insignificant in comparison. We think things like "I don't have that kind of anointing," "I don't know enough to share my faith with others," or "I could never look, sound or speak as polished as _____." When we do that, we as a church lose hope that we, the little guys in the pew, can make any sort of difference in a big world. When we compare ourselves to others, we either encourage ourselves with an "I can do that, too!" attitude, or we give up by deciding to leave the mandate of bringing of heaven to earth to the professionals.

Focus!

1 Corinthians 13 is often called The Love Chapter. It ends by telling us in verse 13 that faith, hope, and love remain. I've heard many messages on faith and even more on love, but not so many on hope. And yet, hope is listed among the things that remain. It is one of the attributes of the Kingdom that will endure, so it seems worth searching out.

I'm so grateful that the Bible is full of stories about real life people. Reading about their experiences with a faithful God gives me hope that I can expect the One who never changes to be faithful to me, as well. Sometimes, though, we read the testimony of their exploits with God and then reduce them to mere formulas. It doesn't take long for us to decide that we could never fulfill the requirements of said formula. We might look at Moses, for instance, and decide that we would never be able follow God as he did. We lose our hope and stop trying.

Hebrews 11 lists for us many of the men and women of faith who lived long ago, along with a brief synopsis of how they ran their race. Imagine being as obedient as Abel, who brought a sacrifice that cost him dearly, or having the faith of Noah, who spent years building a boat in the desert at God's command. We are reminded of Enoch, who "walked with God" and then "was no more;" it appears that he walked right into heaven without dying first! (Now that's a good walk!)

Abraham was willing to follow God without knowing where he was going. Does that inspire you to run your race as he did, or does it make you want to give up? The answer depends on where your focus is. When I take my eyes off myself and put them back on the finish line, my hope of finishing my race well is renewed. With Jesus as the finish line, the focus of your race, you can stir up hope that, like Abraham, you will become a friend of God.

And Sarah, dear Sarah who longed to give birth to Abraham's child! When she was old and childbearing was impossible for her, she became pregnant at God's word. She bore Isaac, fulfilling the promise that He had made to her years before. Focusing on the prize of knowing God and making Him known creates a testimony like Sarah's and gives us hope that God will fulfill His promises to us, just as He did hers, even when it seems impossible.

Hope Saved a Baby, Therefore A Nation

Do you know anyone with the courage of Moses' mother? I've thought about her many times and am still amazed by the way she held onto hope in the midst of the terror around her. The story, as told in the book of Exodus, has been the subject of movies such as The Ten Commandments, starring Charlton Heston, and DreamWorks' animated The Prince of Egypt. When we hear a story over and over it's easy to gloss over it, so let's take a closer look at how much hope Moses' mother needed in order to save her son's life.

The first chapter of Exodus tells us that the Israelites had become

Walking In Hope

a great nation, multiplying until "the land was filled with them" (verse 7). This concerned the new king of Egypt greatly, because he was afraid the Israelites would join the enemies of Egypt and fight against him. His initial solution was to make slaves of the Israelites, using them to build great cities, but the more he oppressed them, the more they increased in number. It's impossible to stop the plan of God

Pharaoh's next solution is chilling: he spoke to the Hebrew midwives, instructing them to kill baby boys as they were born. The midwives feared God and refused to obey the order, telling Pharaoh that the Hebrew women were so healthy that they were delivering their children before the midwives arrived. Partial-birth abortion was stayed because of these courageous women who refused to go along with it.

Frustrated by the failure of his first two solutions to the problem of the Hebrews, Pharaoh allowed fear and desperation to govern him, and his next decision was another bad one. He ordered that every son born to the Israelites was to be thrown in the river.

The story then shifts to the household of an Israelite family. We aren't told their names, but we are told that the wife gave birth to a son. "And when she saw that he was a beautiful child, she hid him three months." (Exodus 2:2) Can you even begin to imagine the terror that this couple lived through? The pounding of soldiers' feet, the screams of families as their newborn boys were torn out of their arms and thrown into the crocodile-infested Nile River? The challenge of keeping a newborn or infant so quiet that no one knew he existed? And all of this while living in slave quarters, known not to be private or soundproof!

When Moses' mother knew that she could no longer hide him, she carried out a plan that she'd surely been weaving in her mind day and night for months: she waterproofed a basket, placed her baby in it and put the basket in the river. In a great cosmic irony, the very river that Pharaoh used to kill Hebrew babies became Moses' deliverance when Pharaoh's daughter found him in the water and raised him as her own son.

The tale is recounted factually, without emotion, in Exodus. We find the key to understanding this family's courage from Hebrews 11:23: "By faith, Moses, when he was born, was hidden three months by his parents, because they saw he was a beautiful child; and they were not afraid of the king's command." (Italics mine.)

How could this have been possible? How could parents not have been terrified, living in under the reign of such terror? The key is in the first two words of the Hebrews 11:23 text: "by faith." This same chapter starts with the words, "Now faith is the substance of things hoped for, the evidence of things not seen" (Hebrews 11:1). Faith has a substance — the substance of things hoped for. Moses' parents saw, by faith, that in giving them a son in what appeared to be the worst time in history, God had good plans for them. Their faith gave them hope, and hope gave them courage. They weren't afraid, because fear and hope are like oil and water: they just don't mix. Their hope rose to the top in their emotion tank, and their son Moses, the great deliverer of the Old Testament, lived to run his own race well.

To me, this story is a classic example of walking by faith and running the race well. Despite what was happening around them, the character of God fueled their hope. This couple kept their eyes on the goal and saw God's promises fulfilled.

The Great Cloud

The list of Bible heroes is extensive, and the list of inspirational race runners living among us today grows with each passing day. Now, our race is evaluated by such measurements as whether or not we love God more today than we did yesterday. Are we hungrier for His word this week than last? Has communication with Him (prayer) become more natural as we run our race of faith?

As we walk daily with Jesus, we gain spiritual strength and stamina. On the days when our walk feels like a crawl, we find hope by recounting the testimonies of others who have run their race well. Because the nature of hope is eternal, (1 Corinthians 13), I should never stop hoping. Even if what I've prayed for, hoped for, longed for, believed for hasn't yet happened in the way or time I thought it would or should, the miracle of hope is that hope remains. It hangs around the house and keeps me looking for the answer, the solution, the breakthrough. If I don't get what I expected today, hope tells me that victory may be just around the bend. It could come tomorrow! This is not a Pollyanna, hide-your-head-in-the-sand kind of theory. This is what hope is and does: it enables me to keep running my faith race when I want to quit. Hope reminds me to keep my chin up and my feet moving. It's the nature of hope to remain and to sustain, not to disappoint. Hope enables me to be unafraid, even in the midst of terror.

It is hope that pulls me out of my slump of disappointment and small thinking, puts me on my feet so I can walk, and gives me courage to believe that I, even I, can run this race and win the gold. Hope calls me to be and do more than I thought possible, even if it involves the word "run."

Just yesterday, in fact, I ran further along the trail than ever before. I felt a bit like Roger Bannister because I'd broken through my own limitations. There was a definite limit to how far I thought I could run, but I ran further than that.

My bluebird friends weren't around, but I could imagine the great cloud of witnesses from Hebrews 12 cheering me on, which got me to thinking about how very much we need each other on this walk of faith. Imagine: instead of bluebirds chirping out encouragement, it could be King David shouting from the balcony of heaven, "Face your giant!" or John, the Beloved, encouraging us to keep our eyes on Jesus' face. What if Deborah, herself, were clapping for us as she watches us listen for Papa's voice and courageously declare His hope to a world consumed by fear?

Hebrews 12:1-2 says it like this:

> *Therefore we also, since we are surrounded by so great a cloud of witnesses, let us lay aside every weight, and the sin which so easily ensnares us, and let **us run with endurance that race that is set before us, looking unto Jesus,** the author and finisher of our faith, who for the joy that was set before Him endured the cross, despising the shame, and has sat down at the right hand of the throne of God.*
>
> (Emphasis mine)

Now, if you'll excuse me for a moment, I'm going to put on my socks and made-for-walking shoes, and then head back to the trail. Perhaps that young man at the shoe store was prophesying over me without knowing it — not what is, but what is possible in my life. Next time I think I'll buy running shoes, after all. And if you see a flash on the trail, don't be concerned. It will just be me, flying by.

TEN

The Community We Live In

Justice at its best is love correcting everything that stands against love.

Martin Luther King, Jr.

There is nothing in the story of Deborah to make us think that she enjoyed conflict or wanted war, but when God said that it was time to make a move, she didn't hesitate. Barak was willing to go if she went, and Jael's courage was certainly stoked by knowing that Sisera was the only enemy left standing.

Situations arise that will bring out the hero in each of us if we're willing to stand up for what is right. Today, as in all days, the world is longing for someone who will take a stand for truth and justice and put a stake in the ground to declare, "No more!" to sin and its consequences. It is time for modern Deborahs all over the land to awaken themselves and take a stand for righteousness by pouring out their lives for the benefit of others. It all boils down to our loving one another as Christ has loved us.

While working on this manuscript, I've been reading a book that I've wanted to read for many years. One of the finest works I've ever encountered, it is fanning a flame that was already burning fiercely in me before I read it: the abolition of sex slavery. The book: *Uncle Tom's Cabin* by Harriet Beecher Stowe, written in 1861.

A passage I read in chapter 16 confirmed to me that slavery is slavery, no matter what form it takes or the time and situation in which it presents itself, and justice is tied to knowing God as Father. The scene I'm referencing here centers around a discussion between a kind, indulgent slave holder and his wife. He is relating to her the manner in which he had dealt with one of his slaves who had been wearing the master's clothes and cologne-water in an effort to imitate and be like him. The master's way of disciplining the slave? "… I had to talk to him like a father, to bring him round." This epoch book decrying human slavery presses the point of needing to know Father. The revelation of God as Father is the hope we have that liberty and justice will prevail again in our day.

Imitating Daddy

What children don't want to be like their dads? For better or worse, we seem to come from our Maker with a built-in desire to imitate our fathers. For those who have never known their earthly fathers or those whose dads inflicted pain on their children, a revelation of Father God's heart brings healing and identity. It is for us, the children of God, to cry out for an outpouring of supernatural encounters with the Lord as Father for those still caught in the slavery of sin.

Following Jesus' baptism, the Father spoke from heaven that this was His son and that He was well pleased with Him. Immediately afterward, Jesus was led into the wilderness to be tempted, and His identity — God's declared words of sonship — were what Jesus carried into the wilderness with Him. They, along with the Word of God that He had hidden in His heart, sustained Him through temptation and led Him to victory. If Jesus needed to hear God's affirming word of sonship and carry the Word deep in His heart and mind, how much more do we?

Living Together in Freedom

The book of Judges draws our attention to a recurring theme: God rescues His people from their backslidden state by raising up a judge to lead them to freedom, and the people then turn their backs on Him once again, repeating the cycle of going from bondage to freedom and back to bondage again. This reminds us that what we do with our freedom is important.

It is critical for us to learn how to steward the freedom we've been given as we welcome others to join us there. As children of God who will soon witness many thousands of people meeting the Father for the first time or coming back to His love, we can use Deborah's story as an example of how important it is to access the wisdom of heaven for preparation strategies. We will also need to hone our relational skills to live in harmony and peace with one another in "full tents."

Galatians 5:13-15 in the Message Bible reads like this:

It is absolutely clear that God has called you to a free life. Just make sure you don't use this freedom as an excuse to do whatever you want to do and destroy your freedom. Rather, use your freedom to serve one another in love; that's how freedom grows. For everything you know about God's Word is summed up in a single sentence: Love others as you love yourself. That's an act of true freedom. If you bite and ravage each other, watch out – in no time at all you will be annihilating each other, and where will your precious freedom be then?

Jesus told us in Matthew 22:39 that the second great commandment is to "love your neighbor as yourself." Again, our vision will be tested as we live in a day of an unclouded sun. We can choose to focus on what is wrong and limiting, which will lead us back to wearing yokes of comparison and envy, or we can seek God's call and destiny in ourselves and others, unlocking and releasing Kingdom dreams and goals.

Taking Down the Fence

I was recently ministering to a woman who was trying valiantly to see the best in her husband. Over and over she repeated, "I'm not offended. I won't be offended by his actions and words." As she spoke, I had a vision of her holding a fence (a play on the word "offence") in her hands. She had a tight grip on this fence, and even as she was speaking to me, I could see that she was deciding whether or not to keep the fence as a barrier between her and her husband. I told her what I saw, and there was relief in her voice as she admitted that she was still deciding. She said to me, "It's a matter of choice. Every time, we have to choose." She was right. Do we stake our ground and put up a fence to separate ourselves from others, or do we let go "of fence," thereby freeing our hands to receive what God wants to give us? To embrace and bring in the harvest — to live in unity and community with our new family members in the body of Christ — we will need to let go "of fence" over and over, and we will need heaven's wisdom to work through challenges that threaten our freedom in Christ.

> *My counsel is this: Live freely, animated and motivated by God's Spirit. Then you won't feed the compulsion of selfishness. For there is a root of sinful self-interest in us that is at odds with a free spirit, just as the free spirit is incompatible with selfishness.*
> MSG, Galatians 5: 16, 17

Captivated

As the church begins to hear and then sing the new songs of the Kingdom, the lost will be come running home. No longer confined to four walls of a building, we will tune our ears to hear where Papa wants us to be and with whom we are to share our song. These new babes coming into the family will not hesitate to join in the song of the Lamb; they will exuberantly sing the songs of freedom. Former captives will be captivated by His face: they will love Him in childlike openness, vulnerability and innocence, and worship Him in the full light of day.

People once caught in a web of sin or terror will hear Papa God call them by name. When they hear this new sound — the sound of His voice declaring their identity — their captivity will be transformed into the freedom of being seized with love and adoration for the One their heart loves. What a day — what marvelous days — those will be! The harvest of souls captivated by God's love displayed through His people. Jesus said, "A new commandment I give to you, that should love one another; as I have loved you, that you also love one another. By this all will know that you are My disciples, if you have love for one another" (John 3:34-35).

The Invitations Being Sent

A world-wide invitation was sent long ago for "whosever" to come home and know God as Father. As more and more people from every nation accept the offer of adoption, we will have the great honor of understanding more of God's character and vastness, of seeing His glory displayed in a variety of cultures, languages, customs and skin colors. What a fascinating neighborhood it will be!

Jesus prayed, "Our Father...Your Kingdom come...," so we know that the Kingdom is a family concern. This Kingdom has a Father. Learning to live together and to trust one another will be based in part on learning to trust spiritual fathers and mothers once again. Malachi 4:6 foretells that in the days of the Kingdom of God, the hearts of fathers will be turned back to the children, and the hearts of the children back to the fathers. We see that happening in both the apostolic movement (true fathers being restored to the church) and in the natural. I remember during the 1970's the "generation gap" being heralded constantly, almost as if families were looking for an excuse not to get along. Today I see parents and their children being good friends while maintaining healthy boundaries of honor within the parent/child relationship. Have you noticed how very involved young dads are with their children in this generation? I see it as a sign of the restoration of fathers on all levels. Seeing both natural families and the family of God being made whole gives great hope to all who have lived life as orphans and to those who have not known Whose they are or where they belong.

Many will accept the invitation to join the Kingdom where people are known for their love for one another. In this community of sons and daughters, we will be humble enough to learn from one another and applaud one another's successes. We will willingly "go low to go high" as we serve one another with gladness.

Living to the Utmost

In his classic devotional book, My Utmost for His Highest, Oswald Chambers writes:

> *Everyone has natural affections – some people we like and others we don't like. Yet we must never let those likes and dislikes rule our Christian life. "If we walk in the light as He is in the light, we have fellowship with one another" (1 John 1:7), even those toward whom we have no affection.*
>
> *The example our Lord gave us here is not that of a good person, or even of a good Christian, but of God Himself. "...be perfect, just as your father in heaven is perfect." In other words, simply show to the other person what God has shown to you.*
>
> *The true expression of Christian character is not in good-doing, but in God-likeness. If the Spirit of God has transformed you within, you will exhibit divine characteristics in your life, not just good human characteristics. God's life in us expresses itself as God's life, not as human life trying to be godly. The secret of a Christian's life is that the supernatural becomes natural in him as a result of the grace of God....*
>
> (September 20, An Updated Edition in Today's Language, edited by James Reimann)

Super What?

Jesus has already defeated Satan; the church is His voice and enforces His victory here on earth. No matter what the terror we face — cancer, depression, difficult finances, bullying, drug abuse — there is peace in God's presence and in His voice. Deborah's walk on this earth made a difference; so does yours. Her voice was strategic and powerful; so is yours. Because Holy Spirit brings truth to life in our hearts, it is imperative that our directives come from the heart of God through His Word. It won't be enough to live out of "good-doing," as Chambers wrote. "God-likeness is the goal we run toward."

As the great numbers of people coming to salvation in Jesus will dictate, each of us as individuals, as families and as the Body of Christ will be stretched, and our spheres of influence will expand. If we stay connected to Jesus while we work as part of a healthy, harmonious Body of Christ, we will have what it takes.

We dare not confuse superhuman with supernatural. Superhuman is found in the movies; it comes from man's determination, mind and ambition, which is not what Kingdom living requires of us. Rather, we are to be supernatural — more than natural, over and above and beyond natural. How do we do that? By remembering Whose we are and the name with which He has identified us, we will do what Jesus did, and even greater things, which for God's children seems only natural. 1 John 4:17 says, "… because as He is, so are we in this world."

Look at the description of this in The Message:

This is why the fulfillment of God's promise depends entirely on trusting God and His way, and then simply embracing him and what he does. God's promise arrives as pure gift.

Our identity is not in what we have done or not done: it's in Him and what He has done.

We call Abraham "father" not because he got God's attention by living like a saint, but because God made something out of Abraham when he was a nobody.

Abraham didn't focus on his own impotence and say, "It's

hopeless. This hundred-year-old body could never father a child." Nor did he survey Sarah's decades of infertility and give up. He didn't tiptoe around God's promises asking cautiously skeptical questions. He plunged into the promise and came up strong, ready for God, sure that God would make good on what He said. That's why it is said, "Abraham was declared fit before God by trusting God to set him right." But it's not just Abraham; it's also us! The same thing gets said about us when we embrace and believe the One who brought Jesus to life when the conditions were equally hopeless. The sacrificed Jesus made us fit for God, set us right with God.

Romans 4:16-25

This compelling love of the Father, this safety and comfort of belonging in His heart as His adopted child, this faith that is available to each of us as we live in hope — these are the identifying marks of the children of God. We who have been shown so great a love will not be able to keep it to ourselves, but will share it freely, because in knowing Papa there is no fear. The time for a demonstration of the love and power of God is now, and we can start by laying our lives down in love for one another.

True Friends Lay Down Their Lives

The following is a story of Kingdom courage unlike any I have witnessed before or since. A girl I'll name Hannah (I never did know her actual name) had run away from a child soldier camp where she had been sold by her father when she was 5 years old. Now in her early 20's, she had finally found a way to escape to a neighboring nation, where we were introduced to her. Years of abuse had left their mark on her bearing, which was that of a much older woman. But the love of Jesus, Whom she met when she arrived in her country of refuge, had brought healing and freedom in striking ways: her ability to laugh and play, her love of worship and the Word of God, and most of all her determination to return to her hometown with the gospel of the Kingdom of God. We actually tried to talk her out of going, knowing that if she were seen by authorities she would instantly be arrested, beaten and taken back to the camp. She would not be deterred, however, because her love was the tent peg that she used to secure hope for her family and village.

I journaled what follows as my husband and I were on our way across a rugged mountain pass in a rickety old van. We'd gone to the border region to pray, and amazingly, we met Hannah's bus as she was heading home. We had thought that we'd never see her again, so this fleeting, unexpected encounter was deeply emotional. In the story is an example of what the community of faith looks like, and as you read it, you will see the hope that comes from falling in love with the Son.

> When Love Becomes our Tent Peg
>
> *"There she is! It's Hannah!" Chaos erupted suddenly as necks craned, arms waved and smiles beamed. Our hands threw exaggerated kisses to our young friend in the bus that was inching its way past our stopped van. What a moment earlier had been the frustration of being blocked once again by boulders on the one-lane mud trail through the mountain pass now took on the sense of a divine appointment as we caught this glimpse of Hannah in the bus bouncing by.*
>
> *She spotted us before we saw her. In fact, I'd dare say that she'd been looking for our vehicle since leaving town six hours earlier. And there we all were — in an improbable spot on a remote mountainside, our love and concern*

for her leaking from our eyes as we waved our love and encouragement. With her long hair pulled back in a traditional tight ponytail, she was leaning out the window as far as she dared, waving and blowing kisses of her own. Her smile was overshadowed by the concern in her eyes and the worry-crease on her brow. Hannah was going home.

"Home" for Hannah is a region of the world where much of the world's heroin is produced. It is a place where sin abounds: young girls are trafficked as prostitutes, and children, often but not exclusively orphans, are captured to become child soldiers. It is a place where this beautiful 20-something woman has lived through horrors that most of us don't even know exist, and where her parents tell her she's ugly and stupid and doesn't love them or she'd help with the drug running. In fact, as the fifth daughter of a peasant couple, her father sold her as a small child to the military camp. If the wrong person sees and reports her as she returns now, she will be conscripted back into the army, beaten and worse for having run away. Home for Hannah is a bit of hell on earth.

A few years ago Hannah escaped the terror her parents had sold her into and made her way to freedom. When she stopped running, she found herself among people who had given up all the world holds dear to be available to tell her of a Savior named Jesus. When Hannah heard that He came because of real love, to set the prisoners free, she gave Him all that she is. Hannah ran into the arms of Jesus, because when sin abounds, grace abounds much more.

The mountain road where we met unexpectedly on that day in June was nothing more than a precarious path being chiseled into the mountainside. Rain had been falling off and on for days, and the red clay mud was a slimy, sticky mess that made traveling dangerous. There was no guard rail or shoulder between the vehicles and the steep cliff, but it was the only road between the town where we'd met Hannah and her home. There was only one way to go, and neither danger nor fear were new to her.

The difference this time was that Hannah was choosing to go home. She had purposely put herself on that bus, knowing that the dangerous road would be the least of the trials she would face. "Why?" we asked her. "Why go home when you know the abuse and pain and fear that await you there?"

"Because they are my family, and if I don't tell them about Jesus, maybe no one ever will. Then they will have no chance to find Him as I have. I'm not afraid, even though I know what could await me. I read Romans 8:35-39, and Holy Spirit told me there's nothing my family or evil men can do to me that will keep God from loving me and being with me. I must go home so my family can have a chance to be free in Jesus. Don't worry about me, but please pray for me."

Yes, Hannah, we will pray. You taught us so much in just one week of knowing you. What an honor to be part of the same family with you, in God. You have stretched us to walk out our faith in ways we've not yet considered.

Dear friends, would you please stop right now, read Romans 8:35-39 and say a prayer for Hannah? You haven't met her in person, but trust me, Papa will know just who you mean. She looks a lot like His Son.

Who shall separate us from the love of Christ? Shall

tribulation, or distress, or persecution, or famine, or nakedness, or sword?

As it is written, "For Your sake we are killed all day long; we are accounted as sheep for the slaughter."

Yet in all these things we are more than conquerors through Him who loved us.

For I am persuaded that neither death nor life, nor angels nor principalities nor powers, nor things present nor things to come, nor height nor depth, nor any other created thing, shall be able to separate us from the love of God which is in Christ Jesus our Lord.

Romans 8:35-39

Falling in love with the Son of God makes champions of us all. Knowing we can't be separated from His love for us gives us courage. Imitating our Father, who IS Love, enables us to live together in community where faith, hope, and love never end.

ELEVEN

An Unclouded Sun

What does it mean that God is omnipotent? Nothing can stop Him from being good to us.

Jake Shelatz

A religious mind sees God as far away, hard to know and difficult to please, as a taskmaster under a brutal sun or a distant old man interested only in disciplining us. But Jesus came to reveal the father, to uncloud the sun so that we can look Him full in the face, without shame. He wants us to see Him not just as a God of Justice, but as our Father who is love.

Deborah's Song

In 2007 I was minding my own business when the Lord spoke to me. He was clear and loud, but I tried not to hear Him. In fact, I argued with myself, trying to convince myself that it wasn't He who

An Unclouded Sun

was speaking to my heart. Turned out it was Him, asking me to start a women's ministry. Whoa! Convinced that He dialed my number by mistake (meaning to call Beth Moore), I gave Him all the reasons that this wasn't be a good idea. He didn't seem to care about my excuses, and instead began downloading to me the outline of what I was to teach.

One of the focuses He gave me was the story of Deborah. I'd read it many times before; it was one of my favorite Bible stories, but when the Lord told me to focus on it, I began reading and rereading, time and time again, hoping to glean from His heart what He wanted me to share.

At the end of Judges 5, which is the song of Deborah, a few verses are dedicated Sisera's mother. You'll remember that Sisera was having carpet time on Jael's tent floor the last time we heard of him. This is how Deborah describes the scene at the home of Sisera's mother, following the historic battle that had just taken place:

> *The mother of Sisera looked through the window, And cried out through the lattice, "Why is his chariot so long in coming? Why tarries the clatter of his chariots?" Her wisest ladies answered her, Yes, she answered herself, "Are they not finding and dividing the spoil: To every man a girl or two; For Sisera, plunder of dyed garments, Plunder of garments embroidered and dyed, Two pieces of dyed embroidery for the neck of the looter?"*
>
> Judges 5:28-30

Isn't it interesting that even the "bad guy" in the story had someone waiting and watching at home for him? It's a good reminder that Satan is our enemy — not people. Even Sisera was a man whom someone cared about.

As I read this over and over, I could imagine brightly colored scarves being twirled in the air in a victory dance, jauntily wrapped around the necks of the victors. In fact, the Word says two scarves, and I can just imagine the joyful, carnival-like atmosphere of crowds celebrating their victorious troops coming home. Can't you?

Even though I know that this didn't happen for Sisera, the passage made me think about wrapping scarves around necks and joy and — well, it made me think of the prodigal son. Okay, I realize that's quite a leap, so I'll be glad to explain.

When The Orphan-Hearted Come Home

Luke 15 records Jesus' telling of the prodigal son, a story of great depth with many layers of truth. A father had two sons. The younger asked for his inheritance, and when the father gave it to him, the son left home and spent it foolishly on wild living. A famine came to the land, and having spent all he'd been given, the boy was grateful for a job feeding pigs as he ate of the scraps he fed them. One day he "woke up" to what he'd become and decided to humble himself, go home and ask his father to take him on as a hired servant.

Several fine points lie hidden in just this much of the story. I've lived in an area where large numbers of hogs are raised, and like anyone who has ever experienced their rank odor, I can tell you that it's not a smell that one soon forgets. If a person spends any length of time near hogs, the stench of them clings to his clothing and even gets into his skin and hair. It takes a lot to get rid of the smell of pigs. While it's not something I can prove, I'm thinking that this young man probably didn't shower with Irish Spring soap before coming home. He probably didn't use a good mouthwash, either. (He'd been eating hog slop, remember?) I'm pointing this out because it makes what happened next that much more shocking.

As this young man approached home, his father saw him coming and ran out to greet him. In fact, the Bible says it this way: "But when he was still a great way off, his father saw him and had compassion, and ran and fell on his neck and kissed him" (Luke 15:20). "Fell on his neck" doesn't mean that he tripped and landed on him; it means that he hugged him. Embraced him. He didn't shake his hand or pat him on the back. He hugged him. I had to look that one up.

I found that the word "embrace" comes from a French root meaning "two arms." Some of the definitions include: "to clasp in the arms, hug; cherish, love; encircle, enclose; to take up readily, gladly; to be equal to or equivalent to." Synonyms are "to adopt, include."

The love of the father was so compelling that he didn't take time to consider options, such as having the son clean up before hugging him. His extravagant love ran toward his son and grabbed him up in a two-armed embrace. The son was totally enclosed in the spirit of adoption that was flowing out of the father's heart. The one who came crawling home hoping to be a servant was welcomed as a son with enfolding love.

As soon as I saw this I knew what I needed to do when I held my first meeting: give the women scarves. After teaching some of what I've written in this book, I invited the women to come forward, and my team then presented each one with a scarf — "dyed embroidery for the neck of the victor," if you will. I wanted them to have a symbol of the Heavenly Father's acceptance of our coming to Him just as we are — enfolded in the safety of His embrace and enveloped in the protection that His arms represent. Enveloped. The safe haven of an envelope of Father's love.

This word picture of how God receives us gives me hope for my tomorrows.

A Lover's Embrace

When my team wrapped those scarves around the necks of the women who attended that Women's Advance meeting in Belfast, Northern Ireland, it became obvious that the Lord was using this simple act as a powerful statement about the Father's love. Afterward, one of the women came up to speak with me. She said that she didn't know whether or not women in other places understood the full impact of this gesture, but she was pretty confident that the women there "got it." She told me that nearby was a town named Killinchy, and that when a young woman falls in love, a colloquial saying is, "She's got a Killinchy muffler!" (A muffler is a scarf in British English.) What it means is that she now has a lover's embrace. To their way of thinking, a muffler (scarf) represents a lover's embrace.

By George, I do believe they've got it!

Lifesaving Hope

We need hope the most when we are in the middle of circumstances that appear from our perspective to be hopeless. Hopelessness feels a bit like being in the ocean as wave after wave of pain or trauma hits us in the face. We tread water and try to keep our noses above the rough waters (that is, we try to find hope), but we get so tired. Anyone who has suffered with a loved one through hospitalization, an accident, a missing family member, abuse, financial trouble, etc., knows just what I mean. We can't find the strength to keep treading water, we can't find a life preserver and we can't get ourselves to shore. We can't see a way out of the situation that seems to be drowning us. In such times, we desperately need someone on shore to throw us a life raft of hope.

There's a saying that hope floats, which means that its very nature cannot sink. Certainly it's true that grabbing onto the hope makes it easier to float (rest, trust, have faith) as we endure the rough seas and difficult times. Sometimes a person on shore can pull us out by providing money, practical help or wise counsel, but usually we must wait for a calmer sea. Will surgery be required? Will the lost child be found? Will the husband come home tonight? Waiting is never easy, but when we wait and rest on what we know to be true in God, we float on hope.

Faith, hope and love remain. The greatest is love, but all three remain for all eternity. Love is usually not so hard to express, and faith often remains strong during stressful times, but hope soon dissipates when we are weary. Exhaustion makes everything look too hard, too much, too difficult. Exhaustion makes the possible seem impossible and leads to despair. Rest is the antidote to exhaustion and therefore a way out of hopelessness.

In today's busy world, The Lord is reminding His people that rest is one of His life-saving devices. I've heard it said that most Christians try hard to keep 9 of the 10 Commandments, but that they have made the one about resting on the Sabbath negotiable. Where we have made that true in our own lives, we have done so to our own harm.

Step into Freedom!

A woman's yoke, made of wood, hangs on my office wall. It's about 12 inches long and 5 inches wide, and the ropes for holding a harvest basket are still attached. This particular yoke once belonged to a friend of mine who lives in a remote village in Asia. She, like all the women in her tribe, had a yoke made just for her. It was made to fit snugly without pressing against her neck, and she wove a headband to attach at the top so her forehead could share the weight of the harvest with her stooped back.

At the clear direction of the Lord, I purchased her yoke a number of years ago. When I bought it from her and prayed for her freedom from every bondage that had weighed her down, I felt that it was a prophetic act for multitudes of women who have been and will be set free from sex trafficking around the world. Since that time I have used it numerous times as a show-and-tell demonstration of what it means to carry a yoke.

Once home, I unpacked it, cleaned it up and then decided to try it on for myself. It slid on easily, and I imagined what it would be like to carry the heavy burden of harvest this way.

Because it wasn't something I wanted to wear around for the day, I started to take it off, and to my horror, I couldn't! I couldn't pull it over my head, and because it was made of wood, there was no way to manipulate it. I started to panic a bit, wondering how and why I managed to get myself into this predicament, and wondering what Jim would say when he arrived home and had to saw this thing off my neck!

And then, suddenly it was off, and I was holding it in my hand. Greatly relieved, the understanding of the lesson I'd just learned hit me hard. You see, to get out of the yoke I had to step forward — I literally had to pull it back and away from my neck at the exact same time that I stepped forward, because it was much too narrow at the neck opening to pull up over my ears. I heard God speak to me that all yokes of bondage are the same in this way: we don't free ourselves from them by pulling them over our heads, i.e. through our intellect. The only way to escape from a yoke of bondage is to step forward and walk away from it. Wow.

In Matthew 11:28-30, Jesus speaks to us about yokes and rest. Twice in these three verses He makes it a point to say that He wants us to come out of our bondages (yokes) for the purpose of rest:

Come to Me, all you who labor and are heavy laden, and I will give you rest. Take My yoke upon you and learn from Me, for I am gentle and lowly in heart, and you will find rest for your souls. For My yoke is easy and My burden is light.

I began to realize that some of what slows me down in my life, my 'race', is carrying old ways of doing things. What I mean is this: were I to go to the major cities of the nation where I bought the yoke, not one person there would know what it was, what it was used for or where it came from unless they, themselves, had grown up in a village. People in the cities don't use primitive yokes anymore; they use the trunks of their fully-equipped Audis. They don't go to outdoor markets to buy their produce, but rather to slick, well-lit, modern grocery stores that take credit cards. A yoke is a very old-fashioned way of getting a job done.

What have I done in the past that, while not necessarily wrong, doesn't fit into my future? What do I carry that is cumbersome, awkward and weighs me down? I want to identify those things and step forward, out of old mindsets and into the Kingdom— out of the fog and into an unclouded sun.

Whatever the lists or fears or burdens that we've been carrying on our backs might be, Jesus wants us to step out from under them and into freedom. The reason? He wants us to rest. He's not a slave driver or a harsh CEO. He knows that we need rest, and He offers it freely — rest for our bodies, our minds and our souls. As we remove the burdens that we've accumulated in our "harvest baskets" all these years, we'll be able to walk out of our self-imposed yokes and into His, which He promises is easy and light. When we wear His yoke, our baskets will be empty as we go into the harvest field with Jesus, the Lord of the Harvest, leading the way. An empty basket speaks of a place ready for many spiritual children coming home, and barns prepared to hold a harvest of souls.

The light and easy yoke that Jesus offers is the Kingdom revelation of the Father's love and our identity as His adopted sons and daughters. When we come into this revelation, we accept Jesus' invitation to "labor to enter into rest" and then labor out of His rest. His Kingdom advancement on earth is accelerating, and we're now running faster and further in a day than we ever thought possible. Leaving the old yoke of slavery behind and wearing Jesus' new yoke of belonging in Father's heart, we can run more easily. We'll be able to stay in the race until the end if we run with His easy, light yoke, which is laboring out of our rest in Him. We can rest in our Papa's embrace.

Restful Thoughts

I journaled the following thoughts a couple of years ago when the Lord began helping me step out of my yoke. While I understand that "rest" is not exclusively the absence of physical activity, letting go of busy-ness was my greatest challenge.

> *Rest and freedom = to spend a day doing nothing. That is, nothing to show for it on paper, and have it be honestly, truly, perfectly okay. More than okay — encouraged and applauded. This blows me away and is hard to take.*

> *I come from a world of lists. Do this and do that — as many as can fit on a notebook page, and sometimes I need a second paper. My value has been directly linked to that list, with projects carefully and boldly crossed out as I finished them. Each item that had a pen strike through it was like a notch on my belt to prove to any who would look that I mattered. I counted for something. My life was important*

and I deserved to be among them. The fact that I could provide a list of things "done!" showed and proved, to my mind, that I was needed. After all, how would these things have been accomplished without me? And where would you — my husband, my child, my friend — be, if I weren't here to take care of these things and mark them off my list?

My list was my identity card, proof that I existed and that who I was mattered. It was my passport to acceptance and belonging. The more crossed-off accomplishments on my list, the more precious, valuable, special, unique and worthy of honor they proved me to be.

Most all of this came from between my own two ears and my "orphan heart."

Not all of us have a list of household or yard chores that we use as a passport to self-worth. For some, the notebook paper or iPad app is filled with what they didn't eat or how many pounds they lifted at the gym. Others need a bank ledger, a killer stock market trade or the closing of a big deal. Some people prove their self-worth by obtaining a 4.0 GPA. However an accomplishment list reads, it does not reveal our true value or identity. Please understand that I'm not talking about doing our work with excellence; excellence is a hallmark of the Kingdom. I am describing self-imposed, unrealistic expectations that lead us into the bondage of hopelessness. To judge ourselves by the crossed-out items on a list of accomplishments is to leave ourselves open to disappointment and defeat when we fail to do all that we'd planned.

When we remember who and whose we are, our journey toward freedom and an unclouded sun either begins or resumes. Lists of expectations can never define our worth, and to be unencumbered and undriven by them, whether self-imposed or otherwise, is to be free. Free people have the expectation of a good tomorrow — and that, by definition, is hope.

Hope that Shakes the World

We have the answers. We are the answer to a lost and hungry world. We, who have been adopted into God's family, now have a passion to find other orphans and bring them home to Papa. This won't happen as a result of the eloquence of our speech or the flawless stride of our walk with God, but by a demonstration of Holy Spirit power. For too long the world has looked at a complacent, sleepy church and has been disinterested in the boredom acted out week after week. When the church begins to experience the earthquake of His resurrection power, the same power that released Jesus from the dead, men and women will rush to our doors, just as they did when Paul and Silas's worship brought heaven to earth in their prison cell, calling "What must I do to be saved?"

The physical shaking experienced in the church during recent years has been the precursor to a great spiritual shaking that will awaken the church to God's Kingdom. When God shows up, we won't be able to sleep, although we may act like dead men as we fall in his presence and glory. Hope in God's power will displace hope in the power of man. Believing in, trusting in and hoping in Him produces in us the mindset of over-comers. What we think in our hearts, we are, and as our minds are renewed by being washed in His Word, the dirt and dust of a long dry season will become a memory. Refreshed by the rain showers of His presence, our thoughts will change and our actions will line up with our thoughts — another way to describe repentance. We will be new creatures with rested minds, bodies and souls, free to run our race unencumbered.

Face to Face

In the final verses of the song of Deborah, she declares in song what it is like to be both defeated and victorious. I love the way the Message Bible says it:

> *Thus may all God's enemies perish,* **While His lovers be like the unclouded sun.**
>
> Judges 5:31, Emphasis mine

Radiant God-lovers. Nothing between our face and His. No veil, no shadow, no cloud. No darkness, nothing in the heavens or on earth that can separate us from the intense burning of His look of love.

This is our identity. Our destiny. Our future. Our hope.

TWELVE

The Unstoppable Song Of Hope

The was never a night or a problem that could defeat sunrise or hope.

Bern Williams

He's more brilliant than the sun... My tires seemed to beat a cadence on the uneven tar patches of Highway 218 North. As I watched the day break out of complete darkness and enter the first light of morning, a refrain rolled through my mind: "Here He comes! Here He comes!" Measure by measure, one inch on the vast horizon at a time, the world around me began to glow. The headlights on my car, which moments ago had been penetrating the darkness, were now becoming irrelevant as the brilliance of day broke upon Iowa's freshly harvested cornfields. The dim glow of dawn had been the only evidence of a new morning until the praise songs of birds began to awaken the day. A muted blush on the expansive, flat fields swelled into a warm canopy that seemed to pull the sun up from its nighttime hiding place, and as the sun's heat strengthened, the rhythm of its pulse sent ten thousand warm rays over the land, embracing it into life. Kissed awake, the earth released her cover of night and sprang into day. Unhindered by clouds, the heartbeat of heaven called a land to worship its Creator. A celebration began as creatures great and small awakened, enveloped in the honey-golden glow.

My vehicle became a sanctuary as my soul worshipped. For perhaps the first time in my life, I saw more than a sunrise. I was stirred to my depths by the awareness of His arising that washed over me. This picture, this earthly metaphor of my heavenly Bridegroom arising in full strength and pushing back the darkness to enfold me in acceptance and love, was almost more than my heart could take in.

Another day, full of new mercy, had begun. Goodness and mercy assumed their rightful place as my rearguard, and I traveled down the road into my day, face to face with my God in the full light of day.

The whole world is singing the praises of God, if we only have ears attuned to hear.

Creation Sings

I remember the first time I heard a recording of the sounds made constantly, day after day and eon after eon, by the planets. If you've not yet experienced that, I encourage you to search for a NASA link to the songs that the universe is singing. Prepare to be overwhelmed when you hear the ringing and sighing and deep, resonant tones unique to each of the planets recorded thus far. I was stunned. I was in awe. I am still amazed, and the wonder of it is a sign to me of how every creation of God is tuned to the worship channel.

Sing a Song of Praise

Psalm 19 is labeled as a song of David that he addressed "To the Chief Musician." While commentaries note that the chief musician was the man in charge of worship in the temple, I find it easy to think that David, known for his songs, his voice and his singing, also addressed this song to the One from Whom sound and music originated.

I don't know whether David was in the temple or in the field tending sheep when he wrote Psalm 19, but I do know that his heart was set to worship God. It's as though David wanted not only to express the understanding he had of the Lord and his emotions toward Him, but also to make clear that even his ability to praise had come from the One whose voice and hands had created all. David was not saying that the heavenly bodies are divine, nor is he hinting that they control or reveal anyone's destiny. Rather, he is saying that our creator God is so great that even the heavens themselves cannot help but sing His praise!

His Arising is Like the Sun

In the first six verses of Psalm 19, David says that the created universe itself is a testimony of God's presence and reality.

> *The heavens declare the glory of God;*
> *And the firmament shows His handiwork.*
> *Day unto day utters speech,*
> *And night unto night reveals knowledge.*
> *There is no speech nor language*
> *Where their voice is not heard.*
> *Their line has gone out through all the earth,*
> *And their words to the end of the world.*

In them He has set a tabernacle for the sun,
Which is like a bridegroom coming out of his chamber,
And rejoices like a strong man to run its race.
Its rising is from one end of heaven,
And its circuit to the other end;
And there is nothing hidden from its heat.

Amazing! The heavens — the solar system, the firmament — have a voice! They have words, they utter speech and reveal knowledge, and every language can understand what they are expressing: the glory of God. The heavens, the planets and the stars are seen by all men everywhere. There is no place on earth that does not have access to a view of the heavens above.

And every place on earth has a sunrise.

Experience Goodness and Mercy Following You

Psalm 19 captures so much of what I have endeavored to express about hope. Along with hope, wisdom and understanding are two attributes of God that we will need to navigate our days. Scripture tells us that God declared wisdom into existence. He prepared wisdom, He searched it out, and then He said to man, "The fear of the Lord is wisdom, and to depart from evil is understanding" (Job 28:28). God knew that we would get hung up on what it means to have wisdom and understanding, so He made it as simple as possible for us to grasp: wisdom equals fearing God; understanding equals departing from evil. That seems pretty clear to me.

The lenses (mindsets) through which we view the Lord, ourselves and each other, are critically important, and so is the lens through which we view the world around us. As each of us walks through the personal situations of our lives, we have the opportunity to choose lenses of mercy and to respond with wisdom and understanding, overlaid with hope. It is never too late for His mercy to help us — it's new every morning, not just on the mornings that we deserve it. He stands ready to pardon and forgive, to remake and restore. Micah 7-18-20 says it like this:

> *Who is a God like you, pardoning iniquity and passing over the transgression of the remnant of His heritage? He does not retain His anger forever, because He delights in mercy.*
>
> *He will again have compassion on us, and will subdue our iniquities. You will cast all our iniquities into the depths of the sea.*
>
> *You will give truth to Jacob, and mercy to Abraham, which You swore to our fathers from days of old.*

May the Lord grant us the ability to speak and declare that which is true according to His Word — in other words, to say what we want to see instead of what we do see. He Who created the worlds by speaking created us in His image; therefore our words hold creative power. As we see situations unfold around us, may we speak into them words of life from His heart. If we do that, then the words of our mouths and the meditations of our hearts will indeed be acceptable in His sight.

Strategies that lead to Hope

As surely as the sun rises each morning and sets each evening, the Lord is faithful. It is my prayer that the stories and teachings you've read in this book will encourage you to live each day holding onto hope. As Abraham and Sarah showed us the way to hope against hope, may we remember and believe:

- Knowing that He has named me gives me a future and hope.

- Knowing that the universe is "singing" gives me hope. It tells me that the picture is bigger than the one I see with my eyes.

- Remembering Whose I am keeps hope alive in me by reminding me that I am not alone.

- Tasting of His goodness and enjoying its honey-like sweetness gives me the energy to hope for a good future.

- Rejoicing in the gifts He has given, I am reminded that He will use whatever is in my hands to defeat whatever stands in the way of love.

- Keeping my ears tuned toward Him, I can know and hear my Father's voice. Knowing that He is guiding and protecting me gives me great hope that He is with me.

- Building a bigger tent to receive the harvest of souls, I have hope and assurance that Father is able to increase my capacity to love and serve within the boundaries that He establishes for my life.

- Stepping out of my yoke of busyness and into His rest restores the hope that I can look forward to healthy relationships and a fulfilling community.

- Allowing Father to embrace me as I am, I have the hope that as I press on to be all that I am destined to be, the race I run will bring justice and goodness to a hurting world.

The story of Deborah concludes with a line that is precious in the hope and promise it holds. Verse 31 of chapter 5 ends with this statement: "So the land had rest for forty years." An entire generation set up for peace and success because of the obedience of God's people to respond to His voice, thereby delivering a nation.

This is the legacy I want to hand on to my children and theirs, for generations yet to be born.

Watching, waiting and longing with anticipation, we hope for the day when faith becomes our sight — the day when our lover, the Bridegroom, parts the heavens and appears. All of our deep passions and our desires to belong will find their completion as we, the spotless Bride, are with Him at last, as clear, as clean and as brilliant as an unclouded sun.

Epilogue

When this book began to take shape in my heart a few years ago, I began asking the Lord for His help in expressing what I believe is a word in due season. From an early age I have had a strong conviction that the Word of God is not merely a history book or a religious icon, but rather a book that is living and powerful when it's truths are activated in our lives.

Therefore I've never been one to be content with 'fill-in-the-blank' Bible studies. While they have their place and I've been blessed and taught by doing some, my deeper desire is to read the Bible and then be able, with Holy Spirit's help, to apply the truths I read there to my own life. I thoroughly enjoy reading the historical record and seeing how I can learn from it: I value deeply reading the prophetic and poetic writings and allowing God to bring revelation of His love and plan to life in me.

I am submitting to you the story that got this book started. Having read the account of Deborah and Barak numerous times, this story one day came to life on my computer screen as I typed there what I imagined a 'Deborah' might look like today, in 2012. There are many scenarios that could be written in stead of the one submitted here, but I ask you, my Reader, to ponder what part is yours to play in bringing hope and Kingdom advancement as you read the following depiction of a modern day Deborah. Ask the Lord how a modern Deborah might employ hope in a hurting, dark world. Dare to ask how you can be a Deborah.

May her story cause you to awaken to your destiny. May this rendering of the power of one person to initiate restoration in her family and society bring you courage and vision – and yes, hope.

When Restoration Begins

In the way of most crises, Debbie's seemed to sneak up on her gradually and pounce all at once. The whole town was shocked, for this was not what they expected for the lady who was one of most genuinely thoughtful and kind people in the community.

Debbie was well known because of all the good she did. With seemingly endless energy, she was forever humming a tune or singing a favorite song as she buzzed about helping others. Known to be a faithful, happy wife and mother, her hospitality drew guests to her door. When a job needed doing at the church or the PTA, she was one of the first to volunteer. Food needed? Debbie made some! Costumes needed for the play? Debbie sewed them. Ball team needing a ride to practice? No problem – Debbie gladly provided a ride in her van. Not only did she pick the children up and transport — she also treated them to ice cream on the way home! Was a neighbor sick? Someone in the neighborhood depressed? Everyone called Debbie! She knew what to do; she knew what to say.

Debbie was one of a kind in her town, as she genuinely loved people. It's easy to imagine how people swarmed to her for advice and help, knowing that she wouldn't think of turning them away.

Epilogue

When her usually pleasant son suddenly became surly and emotionally distant the first little red flag began to fly in her mind. She observed that his life-long friends began slipping away as new, rougher and tougher young men started showing up at the house. His new friends came just to give him a ride to town; they never stayed or joined in on family meals or play. "No, nothing's wrong," she reasoned. "He's a young man growing up in a tough area: he'll snap out of it and be fine."

Then, one day a friend who lived down the street called Debbie, panic shaking her voice. Through her neighbor's gasping cries, Debbie was able to make out the message: her friend's son had overdosed on cocaine. Barely able to distinguish between her neighbor's news and the horror smashing into her conscious mind, the little red flag in the back of Debbie's mind suddenly became a flashing red light between her eyes. So many things began to make sense: her own son's late nights, his hushed phone calls, his attitude that kept pulling him further away from his parents' hearts.

When Debbie and her husband confronted their son, the defiance in his voice and hatred in his eyes confirmed their worst fears: an enemy was loose in their own home, their own neighborhood. Tearing families apart, cutting short the lives and destinies of the young that it seemed bent on destroying, this enemy had now raised its head and was no longer hidden in the shadows of darkness and lies. Suddenly the community's tranquil life was shaken to the core, and all its residents realized that they must face and defeat this enemy. For the sake of life as they had known it, for the sake of their very lives and futures, they had to take action.

What this enemy didn't realize was that hidden in Debbie's golden heart was the DNA of a warrior. Not only was she prepared to fight for her son and many like him, but Debbie knew her God, and she knew how to pray. On her knees one minute, up and fighting for her family's stability the next, this woman who had brought honey-like sweetness to so many lives now began to show that she could sting. She aimed her stinger not on people but on the underlying issues of the city's youth: fatherlessness, boredom and a lack of spiritual identity. She began focusing her energy on ending this enemy of drug abuse in her family and her town. Although the core of who she was never changed, Debbie was now like an angry bee that had been swatted at one too many times. Those who stood with her in the battle looked to her for strength and leadership, and they were grateful for her courage. Those who stood in her way soon learned why it's never good to stir up a hornet's nest.

With the order and precision of a general at war, this Mother went to war for her children and others like them. She herself discovered new depths and expressions of her identity as she fought for justice and freedom.

Debbie began living up to the fullness of the meaning of her name: The Bee.

Resources

Finally Free

An overriding message of Brenda's life is that of coming out of bondage and into freedom. Bound by fear and insecurity for much of her life until age 30, she continues to experience the fulfillment of Psalm 124:7, which reads: "Our soul has escaped as a bird from the snare of the fowlers; The snare is broken, and we have escaped." (NKJV)

Finally Free is a ministry born out of a desire to see people break free from that which has held them back from the fullness of their call and destiny. As people are equipped with tools to build their lives on the foundation of the Word of God, many around the world are becoming Finally Free.

The format of *Finally Free*, while continuing to evolve and expand, has been centered around three weekend gatherings, which Brenda calls *Advances*. They are presently structured as such:

The Look of Love   Based on the story of Miriam in the Old Testament, we discover Who God is. Just as Miriam had heard the stories of Him but then saw His power, justice and love in action, we, too, come away with a fresh revelation of this Father of Love that we embrace.

The Potter's Delight   The story of Deborah in the Bible book of Judges gives us the framework for a weekend filled with fresh revelation of how the Lord sees us, His children. Freedom comes as we see ourselves through His eyes.

Adored and Adorned   The preparation Queen Esther went through, as recorded in the book named for her in the Bible, gives us clues as to how we can prepare ourselves to one day meet our Bridegroom. Just as importantly, how we can live in such a way to please Him and honor Him, here and now.

To stay current with the changes *Finally Free* experiences as it grows, and/or to learn more or to contact Brenda for a speaking engagement, please refer to her website at:

www.BrendaVanWinkle.com

BrendaVanWinkle@gmail.com
www.BrendaVanWinkle.blogspot.com

Other Titles by Brenda

In Love, Where I Belong

> *"I'm so glad you wrote this book! Your writing style made it easy for me to enter into your stories, and for the first time, being adopted into God's heart makes sense not only in my head, but my heart. This book needed to be written! I needed to read it."*
>
> ~ from one reader

Brenda's first published work, *In Love, Where I Belong*, is filled with stories that bring the reader into the security of knowing they belong in God's heart.

Having traveled extensively and ministered to people from various nations and backgrounds, the author sees a common theme: We all long for a place where we belong. Each of us is born with an innate desire to be loved, to be wanted, to belong. For many, the journey of seeking that place of belonging leads to a dead-end, as the avenues being sought don't offer life-giving solutions or answers.

In *Love, Where I Belong* is like a life raft in turbulent times. Using the Word of God as her basis, Brenda weaves true-life experiences throughout this book as her gift of story-telling brings the depth of God's deep and unbreakable love for us close up and makes it personal.

Whether you are a long-time Christian who could use a refreshing read or a new or not-yet believer still seeking Truth, In Love, Where I Belong will help bridge the gap between the ache in your soul and the healing in His heart.

You'll want to buy more than one copy, as you'll want to give some away, but not part with your own! Many people use this book as a devotional that they reference time and again.

ThaiAnn Siam, and The Christmas Miracle

"If I'd had this book as a child, it would absolutely have been my favorite!"
                                    ~ from a 22 year old reader

You don't need to be a cat lover to love this delightful book! Based on the true story of a Siamese kitten Brenda had when a child, it's more than a pet story: it's the story of a father's love.

What little girl doesn't long for a kitten of her own to love? Brenda sure did, and found that the barn cats running around their Pennsylvania farm didn't fulfill her desire for a kitten she could love and call her own. Her dad's soft heart, though set against having animals live in the house, was no match for his two little girl's pleas for a housecat, and soon ThaiAnn Siam came to live in their home.

All seemed to finally be happy and complete when suddenly ThaiAnn went missing for days on end. This captivating story will engage your heart as it speaks not only of an earthly father's love, but the love of our Heavenly Father, as well.

A classic in the making, this book will soon be available in hardcover. A children's workbook will also be available. Check out the website at www.brendavanwinkle.com or amazon.com for ordering information.

As Brenda and ThaiAnn's story remind us: *There's nothing that love cannot do!*

Made in the USA
Lexington, KY
01 July 2012